DEATH BY DENIAL

Death by DENIAL

Studies of suicide in gay and lesbian teenagers

GARY REMAFEDI
M.D., M.P.H.
EDITOR

Boston ♦ Alyson Publications, Inc.

A trade paperback original from Alyson Publications, Inc.,
40 Plympton Street, Boston, Massachusetts 02118.
Distributed in England by GMP Publishers,
P.O. Box 247, London N6 4BW, England.

First edition: June 1994

1 2 3 4 5

ISBN 1-55583-260-1

PERMISSIONS

"Gay Male and Lesbian Youth Suicide," by Paul Gibson, L.C.S.W., from the
Report of the Secretary's Task Force on Youth Suicide, Vol. 3. Published in 1989
by the U.S. Department of Health and Human Services.

"Parasuicide, Gender, and Gender Deviance," by Joseph Harry, from the *Journal
of Health and Social Behavior*, Vol. 24, December 1983, pp. 350–361. Reprinted
by permission of the American Sociological Association.

"Suicide among Homosexual Adolescents," by Ronald F.C. Kourany, M.D., from
the *Journal of Homosexuality*, Vol. 13, No. 4, Summer 1987. Copyright © 1987
by The Haworth Press, Inc. Reprinted by permission of The Haworth Press, Inc.

"Violence against Lesbian and Gay Male Youths," by Joyce Hunter, from the
Journal of Interpersonal Violence, Vol. 5, No. 3, September 1990, pp. 295–300.
Copyright © 1990 by Sage Publications, Inc. Reprinted by permission of Sage
Publications, Inc.

"Suicidal Behavior in Adolescent and Young Adult Gay Men," by Stephen G.
Schneider, Ph.D., Norman L. Farberow, Ph.D., and Gabriel N. Kruks, from
Suicide and Life-Threatening Behavior, Vol. 19, No. 4, Winter 1989. Copyright
© 1989 by the American Association of Suicidology. Reprinted by permission of
Guilford Publications, Inc.

"Risk Factors for Attempted Suicide in Gay and Bisexual Youth," by Gary
Remafedi, M.D., M.P.H., James A. Farrow, M.D., and Robert W. Deiser, M.D.,
from *Pediatrics*, Vol. 87, No. 6, June 1991. Copyright © 1991 by the American
Academy of Pediatrics. Reproduced by permission of *Pediatrics*.

"San Diego Suicide Study: Comparison of Gay to Straight Males," by Charles L.
Rich, M.D., Richard C. Fowler, M.D., Deborah Young, M.D., and Mary Blenkush, M.D., from *Suicide and Life-Threatening Behavior*, Vol. 16, No.4, Winter
1986. Copyright © 1986 by the American Association of Suicidology. Reprinted
by permission of Guilford Publications, Inc.

*Making Schools Safe for Gay and Lesbian Youth: Breaking the Silence in Schools
and in Families*, by the Massachusetts Governor's Commission on Gay and
Lesbian Youth. Published in 1993. Publication No. 17296-60-500-2/93-C.R.

Contents

INTRODUCTION:

The State of Knowledge on Gay, Lesbian, and Bisexual Youth Suicide

GARY REMAFEDI, M.D., M.P.H.

Director, Youth and AIDS Projects
Assistant Professor of Pediatrics, University of Minnesota

A connection between suicide and homosexuality has long been recognized in the popular culture,[1] reflected in music (e.g., "The Ode to Billie Joe"), movies (e.g., *The Boys in the Band),* theater (e.g., Hellman's *The Children's Hour),* and other art forms. Yet, few researchers have ventured to explore the link between sexual orientation and self-injury. Early evidence of an association appeared as incidental findings in studies of adult sexuality.[2] They revealed that gay men were much more likely to have attempted suicide than heterosexual men and that their attempts often occurred during adolescence. Newer studies[2,3] have provided consistent evidence of unusually high rates of attempted suicide among gay youth, in the range of 20–30 percent, regardless of geographic and ethnic variability.

In the U.S., suicide is the third leading killer of youth, accounting for 14 percent of all deaths in the teen age-range. For uncertain reasons, teenage suicide rates have risen by more than 200 percent since 1960, as compared to a 17 percent increase in the general population.[4] Surveys of youth have found that 6–13 percent of adolescents have attempted suicide at least once in their lives, but only a small percentage of attempters have received appropriate help.[5]

These disturbing observations have led to considerable epidemiological, psychological, medical, and sociological research to understand the epidemic of self-injury and death among youth. However, the unifying characteristics of young victims are still incompletely understood, despite considerable progress and new information. It appears that adolescent suicide victims are a diverse group. While most have discernible psychiatric symptoms, a sizeable minority have not exhibited psychological or behavioral problems before death. Given the many unanswered questions regarding epidemiological trends and causative factors, no stone should be left unturned by scientists exploring the issues.

Unfortunately, the potentially important link between suicide and homosexuality has been overlooked until recent years for a variety of reasons:

1. Governmental agencies have not adequately supported the study of suicide in homosexual populations. Given the events surrounding the federally commissioned *Report of the Secretary's Task Force on Youth Suicide,*[6] it appears that political forces were at work to suppress the collection or publication of information which has been perceived to benefit homosexual communities.[5] The report's controversial chapter on gay and lesbian youth, included in this book, almost led to a rejection of the whole volume. After considerable debate, the report ultimately was accepted in its entirety, but published only in limited edition.

Commenting on analogous events surrounding the cancellation of a large-scale teen sexuality survey approved by the National Institutes of Health, Gardner[7] has cautioned that governmental agencies can direct the outcome of public policy discussions by channeling the course of scientific study: "The government has pervasive and enduring interests in shaping the conduct and presentation of science, because scientific data from the earth, life, medical, social, and engineering sciences have become essential to the justification of public policy. Important but unfundable topics have a way of never becoming 'serious' science."

Fueling the intrusion of politics into the science, well-funded scholars sometimes oppose new perspectives in their own field of research. Writing in the *New Yorker* magazine,[8] a prominent suicidologist dismissed existing data on the risk of suicide for homosexual youth based on his perception that the participants had been "unusual groups of gays" and criticized activists for using the data to justify social tolerance. He concluded: "Suicide is usually a story of misperceptions and misunderstandings, of feelings of despair and lack of control; it cannot be attributed simply to having a difficult life. And it has no place in anyone's political agenda, no matter how worthy." It is ironic that such critiques of peer-reviewed, published research are aired in popular magazines, rather than submitted to comparable scientific scrutiny. Even more disturbing is the fact that scholars themselves try to foreclose discussion of promising new ideas in defense of their own viewpoints and interests.

2. Another set of impediments to studies of suicide and sexual orientation are the technical challenges. Both are extremely sensitive and controversial subjects, difficult to broach with institutional review boards, professionals, and participants alike. Because adults and, especially, adolescents may keep their sexual orientation hidden, identifying representative samples of gays, lesbians, and bisexuals has been virtually impossible in the climate of American society. Only in the past decade have investigators succeeded in launching research with sizeable samples of gay, lesbian, and bisexual youth, albeit volunteers with unknown biases for participation. Despite the sampling limitations, the works included here by Schneider et al.[3] and Remafedi et al.[2] are important illustrations of the general feasibility of suicide research with homosexual youth.

These studies also have helped clarify that the risk of attempted suicide is not uniformly distributed among homosexual youth, but linked to particular characteristics. Some characteristics resemble familiar risk factors in the general adolescent population, such as family dysfunction,[3] substance abuse, and sexual abuse.[2] Others are unique to studies of gay and bisexual youth: gender atypicality,[2,9] young age at the time of gay identity formation,[3,9] intrapersonal conflict regarding sexuality, and nondisclosure of orientation to others.[3] Although derived from homosexual youth, these data regarding predictions of attempted suicide might help scientists understand other populations as well. For example, the observed relationship between gender nonconformity and attempted suicide may be relevant to any adolescent group, regardless of sexual orientation.

Unraveling the dynamics of attempted suicide among homosexual youth hopefully will lead to better ways to identify young people at risk for completion and to prevent their deaths. Already, the data from homosexual and bisexual youth challenge the psychiatric paradigm that suicide is uniformly related to prior mental illness.

Our own research group[2] was unable to identify any significant connection between attempted suicide and family mental health history, personal psychiatric treatment, or ongoing problems with depression, hopelessness, and suicidal intent. The previously cited works[2,3,9] suggest that social factors may be relatively more important than intrapsychic variables in explaining attempted suicide in gay and bisexual youth.

Such findings bare exciting implications for future prevention efforts. Current curriculum-based prevention programs which aim to educate all students about suicide often miss the youth at greatest risk and generally have proven to be ineffectual.[5] Periodic screening of the entire adolescent population for psychiatric symptoms with the provision of costly treatment is impractical. Alternatively, the identification of high-risk adolescent subgroups by their social characteristics, coupled with opportunities for social support, may prove to be a more manageable and rewarding approach to suicide prevention.

3. A final, noteworthy barrier to the recognition of the risk for suicide among homosexual youth has been the paucity of information about the sexual orientation of actual suicide victims. As previously mentioned, only a small percentage of attempters ultimately will die at their own hands. Suicide attempts are 50–200 times more common than completed suicides.[5] Suicide completers may be a unique subset of all attempters, and data derived from attempters may not be generalizable to those persons who will someday succeed.

In the *Report of the Secretary's Task Force,*[6] Gibson projected that gay and lesbian youth may account for 30 percent of all youth suicides, based on existing data about the prevalence of homosexuality and the relative risk of attempted suicide. Although this alarming and hotly contested figure may indeed be accurate, it will be important for future studies to gather empirical evidence from the psychological autopsies of adolescent suicide victims. In this type of study, health care records, personal documents, and interviews with friends and family members are used retrospectively to reconstruct the circumstances contributing to a suicide death.

In lieu of psychological autopsies, the existing information on attempted suicide for gay youth reflects grave potential for lethality. From the included article by Kourany,[11] we learn that two-thirds of randomly sampled U.S. psychiatrists believed that the self-injurious acts of homosexual adolescents were more serious and lethal than those of heterosexual youth. Moreover, the attempts that my colleagues and I studied were characterized by moderate to high lethality and inaccessibility to rescue in 54 percent and 62 percent of cases, respectively.[2]

To my knowledge, the only psychological autopsy study to examine the sexual orientation of victims systematically has been the work of Rich et al.,[12] also included in this volume. The investigators set out to determine the orientation of adult suicide victims in San Diego County during a specified time frame in the pre-AIDS era. That 10 percent of suicide victims were found to be gay men is impressive, since the proportion of openly gay men in the U.S. is now thought to be less than 10 percent of males. Moreover, since suicide attempts in homosexual persons have been found to be associated with nondisclosure of orientation, it is reasonable to expect that the 10 percent figure is the lowest possible estimate of the actual proportion of gay suicides in the San Diego cohort. Unfortunately, the authors minimized their own findings by overestimating the prevalence of homosexuality in the general population and underestimating the likelihood of missed cases of gay and lesbian suicide.

What lies ahead in the future of research and suicide prevention programs for homosexual youth? From the perspective of research design, studies of suicide attemptors should move beyond the use of volunteers. Future population-based surveys of adolescent health should routinely ascertain the sexual orientation of respondents, thereby enabling analyses of suicide risk (as well as any number of other health problems) in relation to sexual orientation within respective cohorts of youth. However, even with this improved sampling strategy, investigators will continue to wrestle with the validity of self-reported sexual orientation and the generalizability of findings to youth who cannot disclose their feelings honestly.

It is imperative that future psychological autopsies of adolescent victims address the issue of sexual orientation. Surely, this will require an unprecedented collaboration between suicidologists and sexologists to devise appropriate methods to uncover sensitive sexual information from all available sources at the postmortem. Since gay and lesbian youth who complete suicide may not be "out" to families, it will be important to question friends, teachers, and counselors and to examine other variables which indirectly reflect orientation such as manifest gender role, dating behaviors, pornographic materials, diaries and personal artifacts, telephone records, and other novel strategies.

In the future, investigations of attempted and completed suicide should address the issue of suicide risk for young lesbian women. A retrospective review of records from 500 homosexual youth at the Hetrick-Martin Institute in New York found that female victims of violence reported suicide attempts more often than males (41 percent vs. 34 percent).[13] It remains to be determined whether lesbian status itself is a relative protection or a risk factor for suicide. Both Harry[10] and I[2] have found gender nonconformity to be a risk for young men. Is it also true of young lesbians, or can we expect the opposite effect? Answering this question may shed new light on the well-recognized, but poorly understood, gender differences in suicidal behavior in the general population. Females attempt suicide at least three times as often as males; but males are approximately four times as likely to die from an attempt (rate of 18.0 per 100,000 vs. 4.4).[5]

Beyond academic interest, research pertaining to homosexuality and suicide has important implications for clinical practice and public policy. Completed suicides have been found to be associated with other health problems like substance abuse and HIV/AIDS,[14] all of which are overrepresented in gay communities. Understanding and attacking the root causes of self-injurious behavior in the form of suicide may benefit other community health outcomes, too. From a clinical perspective, neglecting the interrelatedness of risky behavior can adversely affect individual young clients. For example, programs offering HIV-antibody counseling and testing to high-risk adolescents should be mindful of their multiple risks for suicide and proceed with caution.

Already, some communities have found sufficient cause to take action on behalf of gay and lesbian youth. Moved by the existing data on the risk of suicide, health professionals and gay and lesbian community members in Massachusetts called for initiatives to meet the needs of youth. Governor Weld responded by establishing a Commission on Gay and Lesbian Youth which issued specific recommendations to families and schools, including protections against discrimination and violence, dissemination of community resources, and education for students, families, and staff. At the swearing-in of commission members, Governor Weld observed:[7]

> We feel strongly that there is a tremendous need to address the difficult issues facing gay and lesbian youth ... Half a million young people attempt suicide every year. Nearly 30% of youth suicides are committed by gays and lesbians ... We must abolish the prejudice and isolation faced by gay and lesbian youth. We need to help them stay at home and in school so they can have healthy and productive lives.

It is left to the individual readers of this book whether or not to approve the governor's findings and course of action.

In preparing this book with Alyson Publications, it has been my intent to stimulate critical thinking about youth suicide and sexual orientation by gathering the existing sources of information for your deliberation. To the best of my knowledge, the book is a complete collection of all the peer-reviewed and previously published journal articles that specifically treat the subject. In addition to scientific articles, two other non-peer-reviewed publications[6,7] have been included because of their historical significance and relative inaccessibility. These various works have been bound together to make their information readily available to researchers, clinicians, students, and interested others.

In my own mind, there is no doubt that the existing evidence points to an inordinate risk of suicide facing homosexual and bisexual youth. Also apparent is the need to expand understanding of the subject. Given what is already known, there is ample reason to earmark research funds for this purpose and to alert human services professionals and students to the current state of knowledge. To ignore the problem now is a missed opportunity to save thousands of young lives, tantamount to sanctioning death by denial.

REFERENCES

1. Rofes, E.E. (1983). *"I thought people like that killed themselves": Lesbians, gay men and suicide.* San Francisco: Grey Fox Press.
2. Remafedi, G., Farrow, J.A., and Deisher, R.W. (1991). Risk factors for attempted suicide in gay and bisexual youth. *Pediatrics, 87*(6), 869–875.

3. Schneider, A.G., Farberow, N.L., and Kruks, G.N. (1989). Suicidal behavior in adolescent and young adult gay men. *Suicide and Life-Threatening Behavior, 19*(4), 381–394.

4. National Center for Health Statistics (1986). *Vital statistics of the United States: Vol. 2. Mortality,* Part A. Hyattsville, MD: Author.

5. Garland, A., and Zigler, E. (1993). Adolescent suicide prevention: Current research and social policy implications. *American Psychologist, 48,* 169–182.

6. U.S. Department of Health and Human Services (1989). *Report of the Secretary's Task Force on Youth Suicide: Vol. 3. Prevention and interventions in youth suicide.* Rockville, MD: Author.

7. The Governor's Commission on Gay and Lesbian Youth (1993). *Making schools safe for gay and lesbian youth: Breaking the silence in schools and in families* (Publication No. 17296-60-500-2/93-C.R.). Boston, MA: Author.

8. Gardner, W., and Wilcox, B.L. (1993). Political intervention in scientific peer review: Research on adolescent sexual behavior. *American Psychologist, 48*(9), 972–983.

9. Shaffer, D. (1993, May 3). Political science. *The New Yorker,* p. 116.

10. Harry, J. (1983, December). Parasuicide, gender, and gender deviance. *Journal of Health and Social Behavior, 24,* 350–361.

11. Kourany, R.F.C. (1987). Suicide among homosexual adolescents. *Journal of Homosexuality, 13*(4), 111–117.

12. Rich, C.L., Fowler, R.C., Young, D., and Blenkush, M. (1986). San Diego suicide study: Comparison of gay to straight males. *Suicide and Life-Threatening Behavior, 16*(4), 448–457.

13. Hunter, J. (1990). Violence against lesbian and gay male youths. *Journal of Interpersonal Violence, 5*(3), 295–300.

14. Marzuk, P.M., Tierney, H., Tardiff, K., et al. (1988). Increased risk of suicide in persons with AIDS. *Journal of the American Medical Association, 259,* 1333–1337.

Gay Male and Lesbian Youth Suicide

PAUL GIBSON, L.C.S.W.

Therapist and Program Consultant, San Francisco, California

From the *Report of the Secretary's Task Force on Youth Suicide*, edited by
Marcia R. Feinleib, Vol. 3: *Prevention and Interventions in Youth Suicide.*
(Rockville, Md.: U.S. Department of Health & Human Services; Public Health Service;
Alcohol, Drug Abuse, and Mental Health Administration, 1989)

SUMMARY: *Gay and lesbian youth belong to two groups at high risk
of suicide: youth and homosexuals. A majority of suicide attempts by
homosexuals occur during their youth, and gay youth are 2 to 3 times
more likely to attempt suicide than other young people. They may
comprise up to 30 percent of completed youth suicides annually. The
earlier youth are aware of their orientation and identify themselves
as gay, the greater the conflicts they have. Gay youth face problems
in accepting themselves due to internalization of a negative self-image and the lack of accurate information about homosexuality during
adolescence. Gay youth face extreme physical and verbal abuse,
rejection, and isolation from family and peers. They often feel totally
alone and socially withdrawn out of fear of adverse consequences. As
a result of these pressures, lesbian and gay youth are more vulnerable
than other youth to psychosocial problems including substance
abuse, chronic depression, school failure, early relationship conflicts,
being forced to leave their families, and having to survive on their
own prematurely. Each of these problems presents a risk factor for
suicidal feelings and behavior among gay, lesbian, bisexual, and
transsexual youth.*

The root of the problem of gay youth suicide is a society that discriminates against and stigmatizes homosexuals while failing to recognize that a substantial number of its youth has a gay or lesbian orientation. Legislation should [be passed] to guarantee homosexuals equal rights in our society. We need to make a conscious effort to promote a positive image of homosexuals at all levels of society that provides gay youth with a diversity of lesbian and gay male adult role models. We each need to take personal responsibility for revising homophobic attitudes and conduct. Families should be educated about the development and positive nature of homosexuality. They must be able to accept their child as gay or lesbian. Schools need to include information about homosexuality in their curriculum and protect gay youth from abuse by peers to ensure they receive an equal education. Helping professionals need to accept and support a homosexual orientation in youth. Social services need to be developed that are sensitive to and reflective of the needs of gay and lesbian youth.

INTRODUCTION

Suicide is the leading cause of death among gay male, lesbian, bisexual, and transsexual youth.* They are part of two populations at serious risk of suicide: sexual minorities and the young. Agency statistics and coroner reports seldom reflect how suicidal behavior is related to sexual orientation or identity issues. The literature on youth suicide has virtually ignored the subject. Research in recent years, however, with homosexual young people and adults has revealed a serious problem with cause for alarm.

Statistical Profile

There is a high rate of suicidality among lesbians and gay men. Jay and Young found that 40 percent of gay males and 39 percent of lesbians surveyed had either attempted or seriously contemplated suicide.[1] Bell and Weinberg similarly found that 35 percent of gay males and 38 percent of lesbians in their study had either seriously

---

* The terms *gay youth* and *gay and lesbian youth* will frequently be used to describe this population in the paper. Transsexual youth are included here because their problems are similar to those experienced by youth who have a minority sexual orientation.

considered or attempted suicide.[2] Homosexuals are far more likely to attempt suicide than are heterosexuals. A majority of these attempts took place in their youth. Bell and Weinberg found that 25 percent of lesbians and 20 percent of gay men had actually attempted suicide. Gay males were 6 times more likely to make an attempt than heterosexual males. Lesbians were more than twice as likely to try committing suicide than the heterosexual women in the study. A majority of the suicide attempts by homosexuals took place at age 20 or younger, with nearly one-third occurring before age 17.

Suicidal behavior by gay and lesbian youth, however, occurs today within the broader context of an epidemic increase in suicide among all young people in our society. Between 1950 and 1980, there was an increase of more than 170 percent in suicides by youth between the ages of 15 and 24.[3] The suicide rate for all age groups rose only 20 percent during that time. At least 5,000 youth now take their lives each year, with the number believed to be significantly higher if deliberate auto accidents, victim precipitated homicides, and inconclusive coroner reports are taken into account. The rate of suicide attempts to completions is much higher among young people than any other age group, with as many as 500,000 attempts annually. This leads us to believe that many times a suicide attempt by a young person is really a cry for help.

Gay and lesbian youth have been a hidden population within the adolescent and young adult age group. Those programs and studies able to document suicidality in gay youth have found they have a high rate of suicidal feelings and behavior that places them at substantially greater risk of taking their own lives compared to other youth (see Appendix A). Statistics from the Institute for the Protection of Gay and Lesbian Youth in New York, the University of Minnesota Adolescent Health Program in Minneapolis, Roesler and Deisher in Seattle, and the Los Angeles Suicide Prevention Center consistently show that 20–35 percent of gay youth interviewed have made suicide attempts.[4,5,6,7] Statistics from Minneapolis, Los Angeles, and San Francisco find that more than 50 percent of gay youth experience suicidality including serious depression and suicidal feelings.[5,7,8] The Larkin Street Youth Center in San Francisco found that among their client population of homeless youth, 65 percent of homosexual/bisexual youth compared to 19 percent of heterosexual youth reported ever being suicidal, and that gay youth had a rate of suicidality nearly 3.5 times greater than other youth.[8] The Los Angeles Suicide Prevention Center, in preliminary data from an unpublished study, found that the suicide attempt rate for gay youth is more than 3 times higher than that of heterosexual youth; their rate of suicidality is more than twice that of other youth.[7]

Why are feelings of self-destructiveness and suicidal behavior so prevalent among gay and lesbian youth? How can we learn to recognize these youth better and help them more effectively in coping with the problems that often lead them to want to take their own lives? The rest of this paper attempts to address these issues by providing an overview of the tasks and problems facing gay youth, an understanding of who they are, factors that place gay youth at risk of suicide, and an approach for society as a whole and the individual helping professional in effectively helping these youth and preventing them from taking their lives.

Tasks of the Gay Adolescent

Gay youth face the double jeopardy of surviving adolescence and developing a positive identity as a lesbian, gay male, bisexual, or transsexual in what is frequently a hostile and condemning environment. Contrary to popular belief, adolescence is not the time of our lives. It is a difficult and complex period of development filled with anxiety and few clear guidelines for helping youth resolve the problems they face, often for the first time, and making the transition to adulthood. Youth are going through physical changes, emotional changes, intellectual changes, and sexual development, all within the context of their particular culture, family, peer group, and capacity as individuals. They must accomplish several formidable tasks, including separating from their families while retaining a core sense of belonging (individuation); learning to form relationships with other people while fitting in with a social structure (socialization); establishing an integrated, positive, individual identity (identity formation); and preparing themselves for the future in an increasingly complex and uncertain world (future orientation).

Problems in accomplishing these tasks play a critical role in the suicidal feelings of any youth but present special hardships for those who are gay or lesbian. First, they must come to understand and accept

themselves in a society that provides them with little positive information about who they are and negative reactions to their inquiries.
Second, they must find support among significant others who frequently reject them. Finally, they must make a social adaptation to
their gay or lesbian identity. They must find where they belong and
how they fit in with a social structure that either offers no guidelines
for doing so or tells them that they have no place.

With the advent of the sexual revolution and gay liberation movement of the past two decades, gay and lesbian youth have been
increasingly aware of their feelings and coming to terms with their
orientation at an earlier age than ever before. This has placed them into
direct conflict with all of the traditional child-rearing institutions and
support systems of our society. Increasingly, this occurs while the
youngsters are still living at home with their family, attending public
school, and developing a sense of their own self-worth in comparison
with their peers and the expectations of society as a whole.

Problems Facing Gay Youth

Lesbian and gay youth are the most invisible and outcast group of
young people with whom you will come into contact. If open about
who they are, they may feel some sense of security within themselves
but face tremendous external conflicts with family and peers. If closed
about who they are, they may be able to "pass" as "straight" in their
communities while facing a tremendous internal struggle to understand and accept themselves. Many gay youth choose to maintain a
facade and hide their true feelings and identity, leading a double life,
rather than confront situations too painful for them. They live in
constant fear of being found out and recognized as gay. The reasons
for their silence are good ones.

Gay youth are the only group of adolescents that face total rejection from their family unit with the prospect of no ongoing support.
Many families are unable to reconcile their child's sexual identity with
moral and religious values. Huckleberry House in San Francisco, a
runaway shelter for adolescents, found that gay and lesbian youth
reported a higher incidence of verbal and physical abuse from parents
and siblings than other youth.[9] They were more often forced to leave
their homes as "pushaways" or "throwaways" rather than running
away on their own. In a study of young gay males, Remafedi found

that half had experienced negative parental response to their sexual orientation, with 26 percent forced to leave home because of conflicts over their sexual identity.[5]

Openly gay and lesbian youth or those "suspected" of being so can expect harassment and abuse in junior high and high schools. The National Gay Task Force, in a nationwide survey, found that 45 percent of gay males and nearly 20 percent of lesbians had experienced verbal or physical assault in secondary schools.[10] The shame of ridicule and fear of attack makes school a fearful place to go, resulting in frequent absences and sometimes academic failure. Remafedi reports 28 percent of his subjects were forced to drop out because of conflicts about their sexual orientation.[5] Gay youth are the only group of adolescents with no peer group to identify with or receive support from. Many report extreme isolation and the loss of close friends.

Gay youth also face discrimination in contacts with the juvenile justice system and foster and group home placements.* Many families and group homes refuse to accept or keep an adolescent if they know he or she is gay. A report by the San Francisco Juvenile Justice Commission found that gay youth stay in detention longer than other youth awaiting placement because of a lack of appropriate program resources.[11] Many programs are unable to address the concerns or affirm the identity of a gay adolescent. They can be subjected to verbal, physical, and even sexual abuse with little recourse. Even sympathetic staff often don't know how to relate to a gay youth or support them in conflicts with other residents. They frequently become isolated, ignored by youth and staff who feel uncomfortable with them. They are easy targets for being blamed and scapegoated as the "source" of the problem in efforts to force them to leave.

The result of this rejection and abuse in all areas of their lives is devastating for lesbian and gay youth, and perhaps the most serious problems they face are emotional ones. When you have been told that you are sick, bad, and wrong for being who you are, you begin to believe it. Gay youth have frequently internalized a negative image of themselves. Those who hide their identity are surrounded by homo-

---

* It is my observation that youth are experiencing more frequent contact with the juvenile court due to (1) increased conflicts in their home communities because of their sexual orientation which require intervention and removal from the home and (2) being open about their sexual identity at an earlier age than before.

phobic attitudes and remarks, often by unknowing family members and peers, that have a profound impact on them. Hank Wilson, founder of the Gay and Lesbian Teachers Coalition in San Francisco, believes these youth constitute a large group who are silently scapegoated, especially vulnerable to being stigmatized, and who develop poor self-esteem.[12] Gay youth become fearful and withdrawn. More than other adolescents, they feel totally alone, often suffering from chronic depression, despairing of life that will always be as painful and hard as the present one.

In response to these overwhelming pressures, gay youth will often use two coping mechanisms which only tend to make their situation worse: substance use and professional help. Lesbian and gay male youth belong to two groups at high risk for substance abuse: homosexuals and adolescents. Rofes found, in a review of the literature, that:

> Lesbians and gay men are at much higher risk than the heterosexual population for alcohol abuse. Approximately 30 percent of both the lesbian and gay male populations have problems with alcoholism.[13]

Substance use often begins in early adolescence when youth first experience conflicts around their sexual orientation. It initially serves the functional purposes of (1) reducing the pain and anxiety of external conflicts and (2) reducing the internal inhibitions of homosexual feelings and behavior. Prolonged substance abuse, however, only contributes to the youth's problems and magnifies suicidal feelings.

Several studies have found that a majority of gay youth received professional help for conflicts usually related to their sexual identity.[5,6] These interventions often worsen conditions for these youth because the therapist or social worker is unwilling to acknowledge or support an adolescent's homosexual identity. Many gay and lesbian youth are still encouraged to "change" their identities while being forced into therapy and mental hospitals under the guise of "treatment."

Those who seek help while hiding their identity often find the source of their conflicts is never resolved because the therapist is unable to approach the subject. This silence is taken as further repudiation of an "illness" that dare not speak its name.

A suicide attempt can be a final cry for help by gay youth in their home community. If the response is hostile or indifferent, they prepare to leave. Alone and frightened, they go to larger cities — hoping to find families and friends to replace the ones that did not want them or could not accept them. The English group The Bronski Beat describes the plight of the gay adolescent in their song "Smalltown Boy":

> Pushed around and kicked around,
>   always the lonely boy
> You were the one they talked about
> Around town as they put you down
> But as hard as they would try
>   just to make you cry
> You would never cry to them
>   —just to your soul
> Runaway, turnaway, runaway,
>   turnaway, runaway[14]

Gay male, lesbian, bisexual, and transsexual youth comprise as many as 25 percent of all youth living on the streets in this country. Here, they enter a further outcast status that presents serious dangers and an even greater risk of suicide. Without an adequate education or vocational training, many are forced to become involved in prostitution in order to survive. They face physical and sexual assaults on a daily basis and constant exposure to sexually transmitted diseases, including AIDS. They often become involved with a small and unstable element of the gay community that offers them little hope for a better life. Their relationships are transitory and untrustworthy. For many street youth, their struggle for survival becomes the fulfillment of a "suicidal script" which sees them engaging in increasingly self-destructive behaviors, including unsafe sexual activity and intravenous drug use. Overwhelmed by the complexities of street life and feeling they have reached the "wrong end of the rainbow," a suicide attempt may result.

While it has become easier in recent years to be a gay male or lesbian adult, it may be harder than ever to be a gay youth. With all of the conflicts they face in accepting themselves, coming out to families and peers, establishing themselves prematurely in independent living, and, for young gay males, confronting the haunting specter of AIDS, there is a growing danger that their lives are becoming a tragic nightmare with living only a small part of dying.

UNDERSTANDING GAY AND LESBIAN YOUTH

Lesbian and gay male youth are young people with a primary attraction to members of the same sex for sexual and intimate relationships. Bisexual youth have an attraction to members of both sexes for sexual and intimate relationships. We use the term *orientation* rather than *preference* to describe this attraction because we still do not know how it originates. We are not certain to what extent genetics, socialization factors, or individual choice determines either a homosexual or a heterosexual orientation. Transsexual youth are young people who believe they have a gender identity that is different from the sex they were born with. This includes young males who believe they are really females mistakenly born in a male body and young females who believe they are really males mistakenly born in a female body. Sexual orientation and gender identity are separate issues for each individual. Transsexuals may have a heterosexual, homosexual, or bisexual orientation. Homosexuals are rarely confused about their gender identity, with lesbians believing they are women and gay males believing they are men.

There are indications that individuals may be predisposed to their sexual orientation from an early age. A gay or lesbian orientation in adolescence is not just a phase the youth is going through. Bell, Weinberg, and Hammersmith found that sexual orientation is likely to be formed by adolescence — even if the youth is not yet sexually active.[15]

Childhood and adolescent homosexuality, especially pronounced homosexual feelings, can not be regarded as just a passing fancy ... [it] seems to be relatively enduring and so deeply rooted that it is likely to continue as a lasting homosexual orientation in adult life.

Huckleberry House found that, when given a choice, adolescents demonstrate a greater degree of conviction than confusion in identifying their sexual orientation, with 75 percent self-reporting as heterosexual, 15 percent homosexual, 5 percent bisexual, and only 5 percent confused or undecided.[9] Most youth who identify as heterosexuals and homosexuals will continue to do so as adults. Youth are more likely to underreport a homosexual orientation because of difficulties in accepting themselves and the fear of a hostile response. Jay and Young found that 56 percent of the lesbian respondents in their survey had previously identified as bisexual, while only 16 percent currently did so.[1] Forty-six percent of the gay males had previously identified as bisexual, while only 20 percent currently did so.

Homosexuality is not a mental illness or disease. It is a natural and healthy expression of human sexuality. In 1935, Sigmund Freud wrote that "homosexuality ... is nothing to be ashamed of, no vice, no degradation, it cannot be classified as an illness."[16] In 1973, the American Psychiatric Association removed homosexuality from the list of psychiatric disorders, and in 1975, the American Psychological Association urged all mental health professionals to remove the stigma of mental illness long associated with a homosexual orientation. In 1983, the American Academy of Pediatrics encouraged physicians to become involved in the care of homosexuals and other young people struggling with the problem of sexual expression.[5] If homosexuality is not an illness or a disorder, it cannot be regarded as such to the extent that it occurs in the young.

Gay and lesbian youth come from all ethnic backgrounds. The ethnicity of gay youth will reflect the ethnicity of youth in your community or seen by your agency. The Institute for the Protection of Gay and Lesbian Youth reports [that] the ethnic breakdown of youth it served matched the population of New York's public school system, with 40 percent black, 35 percent white, 20 percent Hispanic, 2 percent Asian, and 3 percent other.[4] Huckleberry House in San Francisco found that more than half of their overall client population and gay youth seen by the program were ethnic minorities.[9]

There are far more gay youth than you are presently aware of. Kinsey found a significant amount of homosexual behavior among adolescents surveyed, with 28 percent of the males and 17 percent of the females reporting at least one homosexual experience.[17,18] He also found that approximately 13 percent of adult males and 7 percent of adult females had engaged in predominantly homosexual behavior for at least three years prior to his survey. This is where the figure that 10 percent of the population is homosexual comes from. It is difficult to assess the prevalence of a homosexual orientation given our knowledge that sexual behavior actually occurs along a continuum of feelings and experiences. Prevalence is even more difficult to estimate among adolescents because of the complex identity issues with which they are struggling and the scarcity of research on the subject. It is apparent, however, that a substantial minority of youth — perhaps "One in Ten" as one book suggests — have a primary gay male, lesbian, or bisexual orientation. Given the higher rates of suicidal feelings and behavior among gay youth in comparison with other young people, this means that 20–30 percent of all youth suicides may involve gay youth. Parris believes that as many as 3000 gay and lesbian young people may be taking their lives each year.[19]

Coming Out: The Early Stages

Coming out is the process through which a person comes to understand and accept his/her sexual identity and shares it with others. This is seldom a conscious undertaking for heterosexual youth, who find that being "straight" is a given status in our society. It is as automatic as attending school or getting a driver's license. However, identifying oneself as gay or lesbian is a long and painful process that occurs gradually over an extended period of time. Stages in the coming-out process are identified in Appendix B, with the ages reflecting those of gay and lesbian youth whom I worked with at Huckleberry House.[20,21] This population represents the bias of self-identified gay youth seeking services at a runaway program. It is important to recognize, however, that this process begins for many lesbian and gay youth at an early age, with an awareness of their orientation developing by adolescence. It is then that they experience significant conflicts involving understanding of who they are, handling negative reactions from others, and making a social adaptation which can lead to suicidal feelings and behavior. These conflicts must be resolved before the youth can develop a positive identity as a gay male or lesbian.

The first stage in the development of a lesbian or gay identity is an awareness of being different. This often occurs several years prior to puberty, with the youth seldom aware of what this feeling means or how it relates to their sexuality. Lewis, in describing this stage for young lesbians, notes that:

> Because our society and its process of socialization do not include a positive vocabulary for same-sex attractions (whether emotional or erotic), many girls experience only vague, indefinable feelings of "not fitting in."[22]

Bell, Weinberg, and Hammersmith looked at numerous factors (i.e., family relationships) in attempting to determine how individuals develop a homosexual or heterosexual orientation.[15] They provide evidence that this awareness of being different is related to the social roles of the child. During latency age years, the family often reinforces those roles, behaviors, attributes, and interests that are stereotypically associated with being a male or a female in our society. For example, boys are expected to play outside more than girls and girls are expected to stay closer to the house more than boys. Bell et al. found that gay males and lesbians in their study tended to have atypical social roles in childhood that did not conform to gender expectations, while heterosexuals tended to have typical social roles.

> Far fewer homosexual (11%) than heterosexual (70%) men reported having enjoyed boys' activities (e.g., baseball, football) very much.
>
> Fewer of the homosexual (13%) than heterosexual (55%) women said they enjoyed typical girls' activities (e.g., playing house, hopscotch) very much.

This finding held true for a range of variables involving stereotyped male and female roles, with gender nonconformity being the single most accurate indicator in childhood of a future homosexual orientation.[15] However, they add a strong point of clarification for those who would force gender conformity on a child in an effort to "prevent" homosexuality.

> Homosexuality is as deeply ingrained as heterosexuality, so that differences in behaviors or social experiences of pre-homosexual boys and girls and their pre-heterosexual counterparts reflect or express, rather than cause, their eventual homosexual [orientation].

This finding does not account for the substantial percentage of respondents giving answers that were typical for their sexual orientation. Many children, however, who later identify as gay or lesbian begin to realize at this early age that they do not meet the social expectations of their families and other children.

The second stage of the coming-out process is an awareness of being attracted to members of the same sex. This also commonly occurs prior to puberty, with many gay and lesbian youth reporting childhood crushes on other children and adults. Bell et al. found these sexual feelings typically occurred three years or so before any homosexual experiences and appear to be the most crucial stage in the development of adult homosexuality.[15] Most children are unaware of the meaning and implications of these attractions. However, for those who are able to make a connection between their "difference" — homosexual feelings and gay or lesbian identity — depression and suicidal feelings may already be present.

> I always knew that I was gay. When I was 8 or 9 I would steal my mother's *Playgirl* magazines and look at the pictures of men. I also remember seeing heterosexual couples and knowing I wasn't like that. I would get very depressed about not being like other kids. Many times I would take a kitchen knife and press it against my chest, wondering if I should push it all the way in.[23]

Many adolescents experiencing conflicts related to their sexual orientation report having their first homosexual experience around puberty. Some youth, however, first act on their feelings during adolescence. Young lesbians tend to have their first experience at a later age than young gay males.[1] Same-sex play and experimentation is relatively common prior to puberty, with Kinsey reporting that 60 percent of preadolescent boys and 33 percent of preadolescent girls described homosexual play at the time they contributed to the study.[16,17] Pre-homosexual boys and girls often do not have a context in which to put their feelings and experiences. They have learned to hide sexual behavior from adults but have not developed an understanding of the stigma attached to homosexuality. Their initial experiences tend to confirm homosexual feelings. It is now, however, that a terrible thing happens to young people who will have a gay or lesbian orientation — adolescence. Gay and lesbian youth will become distinguished from other youth involved in preadolescent same-sex play by their progress through the developmental stages here identified and the persistence of homosexual feelings and experiences in spite of negative consequences.

Adolescence

With adolescence, many gay and lesbian youth have their first contact with homosexuality, and it is all bad. They are told it is no longer acceptable to engage in sexual behavior with members of the

same sex and that those who do are sick. The only images of homosexuals that society provides them with are derisive stereotypes of
lesbians who are like men and gay men who are like women. Many
experience their first pervasive contact with the fear and hatred of
homosexuality — homophobia.

Nowhere are these harshly negative attitudes toward homosexuality more pronounced than in junior high and high school. These
institutions are the brutal training grounds where traditional social
roles are rigidly reinforced. Boys are going to play sports and drink
beer with the guys. Girls are going to start paying more attention to
their physical appearance in the hopes of attracting boys. Adolescence
will be the last stronghold of these stereotyped roles and behaviors
because young people are looking for identity. Homosexuality and
gender nonconformity are threats to many youth and an easy target for
their fears and anxieties about being "normal."

Youth who have a growing awareness of a gay or lesbian
orientation become painfully aware that they do not fit the "social
script." They see the hostility directed toward homosexuals by
others and hear taunts of "dyke" and "faggot" used indiscriminately
by peers. They become alarmed and realize that they must make
some social adaptation to the situation. Martin describes their
predicament:

> In adolescence, young homosexually oriented persons are faced with
> the growing awareness that they may be among the most despised ...
> As this realization becomes more pressing, they are faced with three
> possible choices: they can hide, they can attempt to change the stigma,
> or they can accept it.[24]

These three adaptations are not mutually exclusive and are often
present in the same individual over time. Many youth initially try to
deny a gay or lesbian orientation to both themselves and others. Those
adolescents who understand and recognize they have a gay orientation
will continue to hide their identity from family and peers for fear of
adverse consequences. Finally, those who become open about their
identity confront those adverse consequences in an effort to win
acceptance and support. Each adaptation contains specific problems
which contribute to suicidal feelings and behavior.

Self-Denial

All young people face tremendous pressures to desist from any homosexual behavior and develop a heterosexual orientation. It is easy to see why adolescents with predominantly homosexual feelings and experiences would try to deny a lesbian or gay identity. They have internalized an image of being a homosexual as wrong and dangerous to their physical and mental health. They have seen the stereotypes of lesbians and gay men, and they don't like them. These youth who don't want to live like that decide they are going to conform to the social roles and start dating members of the opposite sex and become heterosexuals.

Many youth engage in heterosexual behavior in an effort to change their orientation. This often turns out to be a losing battle. Jay and Young found that 83 percent of the lesbians and 66 percent of the gay men in their survey had previously engaged in heterosexual sex.[1] Bell and Weinberg similarly found that 87 percent of lesbians and 68 percent of gay males interviewed had prior heterosexual experiences.[2] Two studies with gay male youth found that at least 50 percent had prior heterosexual experiences.[5,6] Jay and Young add that 55 percent of the lesbians and 46 percent of the gay males reported feeling negative about these experiences. Bell et al., in their study on the development of sexual orientation, conclude that:

> The homosexual men and women in our study were not particularly lacking in heterosexual experiences during their ... adolescent years. They are distinguished from their heterosexual counterparts, however, in finding such experiences ungratifying.[15]

The American Psychiatric Association notes in the 1980 edition of the *Diagnostic and Statistical Manual of Mental Disorders* (DSM III) that "there is a general consensus that spontaneous development of a satisfactory heterosexual adjustment in individuals who previously had a sustained pattern of exclusively homosexual arousal is rare."[25] One potentially serious consequence of this heterosexual experimentation is pregnancy involving young lesbians or gay males that either occurs accidentally or in an effort to "prove" a heterosexual orientation.

Youth who try to change a homosexual orientation and are unable to do so are at high risk of emotional and behavioral problems. They often develop feelings of hatred and rage that can be turned against themselves or others. They may engage in self-destructive behaviors such as substance abuse as an unconscious expression of feelings too painful to face. Others become involved in verbal and physical attacks against other homosexuals as a way of defending against their own fears. Finally, when the youth comes to recognize for the first time that he/she has a primary homosexual orientation, overt suicidal behavior may result.

₹ The DSM III includes a new disorder called "Ego-Dystonic Homosexuality" which describes many of the conflicts faced by youth engaged in denial of homosexual feelings.[25] It is characterized by "a desire to acquire or increase heterosexual arousal ... and a sustained pattern of overt homosexual arousal ... [that is] unwanted and a persistent source of distress." Associated features include guilt, loneliness, shame, anxiety, and depression. Age of onset occurs in "early adolescence when the individual becomes aware that he or she is homosexually aroused and has already internalized negative feelings about homosexuality." The course of the illness indicates that "in time, many individuals ... give up the yearning to become heterosexual and accept themselves as homosexuals ... [with the help] of a supportive homosexual subculture." Remafedi notes that the usefulness of this term is still not known since distress is so prevalent among youth first recognizing a homosexual identity.[5] However, it clearly identifies a phenomena in many young homosexuals that places them at a greater risk of taking their own lives. ;

Those Who Hide

Many youth are aware of their gay or lesbian identity but decide not to be open about it and try to pass as "straight" with their families and peers. They have seen the negative response to homosexuality from society and the brutal treatment of gays by their peers. Sometimes they have been the recipients of verbal or physical abuse as "suspected" homosexuals. Martin believes that hiding is the primary adaptation for gay and lesbian youth.[24] He observes that many realize that their lives are based on a lie, with "the socialization of the gay adolescent becoming a process of deception at all levels, with the ability to play a role." While remaining invisible to others, the pain and loneliness of hiding often causes these youth serious harm to their mental health and social development.

A serious consequence of this adaptation is that these youth suffer their fears and low self-esteem in silence. They are unknown victims of scapegoating with every homophobic assault or remark they witness. They live in perpetual fear that their secret will be discovered. Gay youth become increasingly afraid to associate with others and withdraw socially in an effort to avoid what they perceive as a growing number of dangerous situations. They spend more and more time alone. Aaron Fricke relates the problems of hiding a gay identity in his book *Reflections of a Rock Lobster: A Story about Growing Up Gay.*[26] He describes his response to being victimized by a homophobic assault as he was about to begin high school.

I began to believe that everyone looked down on me and when anyone looked at me I thought I saw their seething hatred of me coming through. When I entered high school I was completely isolated from the world. I had lost all concept of humanity; I had given up all hopes of ever finding love, warmth, or tenderness. I did not lie to myself, but I did keep others from thinking I was homosexual. I could refuse to ever mention my real feelings. That way, I would never again suffer the consequences of being the individual I was. I retreated into my own world.

The only goal left to me in life was to hide anything that could identify me as gay. I became neurotic about this. I once heard that gay people talked with a lisp. I was horrified when I discovered that I had a slight lisp, and it made me self-conscious about how I sounded every time I spoke. Self-doubt set in. I thought that anything I did might somehow reveal my homosexuality, and my morale sank even deeper. The more I tried to safeguard myself from the outside world, the more vulnerable I felt. I withdrew from everyone and slowly formed a shell around myself. Everyone could be a potential threat to me. I resembled a crustacean with no claws; I had my shell for protection yet I would never do anything to hurt someone else. Sitting on a rock under thousands of pounds of pressure, surrounded by my enemies, the most I could hope for was that no one would cause me more harm than my shell could endure.

These youth suffer from chronic depression and are at high risk of attempting suicide when the pressure becomes too much to bear. They may run away from home, with no one understanding why. A suicidal crisis may be precipitated by a minor event which serves as a "last straw" to the youth. A low grade may confirm for the youth that life is a failure. An unwitting homophobic remark by parents may be taken to mean that the youth is no longer loved by them.

Martin also believes this adaptation hinders the social development of gay and lesbian youth.[24] There is an absence of social outlets for gay youth that makes it very difficult for them to meet others like themselves. They shy away from attachments to friends for fear of getting too involved or experiencing rejection. Open relationships or displays of affection with others of the same sex is not tolerated in the gay youth's home and social environment, making extreme secrecy a requirement in developing romantic attachments. (Indeed, these issues form the essence of discrimination against homosexuals in our society.) Consequently, lesbian and gay youth do not learn how to establish and maintain intimate relationships in the way heterosexual youth do.

Young gay males often experience their same-sex relationships as casual sexual contacts with strangers. Because of their age, many of these encounters occur in clandestine meeting places where gay males congregate. Roesler and Deisher found that 76 percent of their subjects had met sexual partners in parks, 62 percent in theaters, and 32 percent in restrooms.[6] Remafedi found that 63 percent of young gay males he surveyed had met other males in gay bars; only 28 percent said they had known their partner for a week prior to having sex.[5] Martin expresses concern that these encounters condition the young gay male to respond to other gay males on a sexual level only.

> He often has not had the opportunity to develop courting behaviors other than direct sexual contact. Heterosexual adolescents learn to date and go through a series of societally ordained procedures with sexual contact as a possible end result. The young gay male often learns to start with the end result, sexual behavior, and then attempts to develop the relationship.[24]

Young gay males face the risk of mistaking sexual feelings for deeper bonds of love. They may despair of the difficulties in forming lasting relationships on the basis of fleeting sexual encounters. Suicidal feelings may follow the failure of casual sex to meet the youth's needs of intimacy and belonging.

Young lesbians are even more isolated than young gay males in their efforts to form intimate relationships. There are few meeting places for lesbians in our society, and casual sexual contacts are a less frequent part of their development. Lewis writes that:

> Because women are socialized to have and maintain relationships, sexual exploration and experimentation often takes place within the context of a relationship.[22]

With fewer social opportunities, however, young lesbians are often not able to form initial relationships with lovers until later adolescence or young adulthood. Suicidal feelings among young lesbians may be due to the extreme isolation they experience and the despair of being unable to meet others like themselves.

Openly Gay and Lesbian Youth

Those who accept their orientation and are open about it with others form a smaller but visible segment of the lesbian and gay male youth population. They learn that only part of developing an identity as a gay male or lesbian is coming to understand and accept our sexual orientation. Now they must find out what their place is and where they belong within the confines of the traditional social structure available to them. There are few role models to emulate and society offers them little support in this process. Gay youth usually don't begin to be open about their orientation until middle to late adolescence.

Many of these youth will have an atypical social role that includes gender nonconformity. Bell et al. found that 62 percent of lesbians surveyed described themselves as "very masculine" while growing up.[15] Remafedi found more than half of young gay males interviewed saw themselves as "less masculine" than their peers.[5] Gender nonconformity may be more pronounced in youth first openly identifying themselves as gay. Sometimes it is a natural and permanent expression of who they are, and sometimes it is a transitional process youth go through in learning that they don't have to behave in any particular way to be gay. Weinberg and Williams found that younger gay males identified themselves as effeminate three times more frequently than did older gay males.[27]

Gender nonconformity in gay youth may reflect natural qualities that do not fit cultural stereotypes (e.g., men who are gentle, women who are strong). Youth may have expressed these attributes since childhood and will continue to do so as adults. Gender nonconformity may also fit the expectations that society sets for gay and lesbian youth. Gay youth are especially susceptible to cultural stereotypes while struggling to find an appropriate identity. One young gay male told me that he literally thought that he had to be "like a girl" because he was gay. There is not a diversity of gay male and lesbian adult role models for gay youth to pattern themselves after. For many young lesbians and gay men, the earliest images of adults they thought were homosexuals were people who fit the traditional stereotypes.

> One young lesbian recalled when she was a child there was a "tough-looking" woman with a slight moustache who drove a pick-up truck and lived on the edge of town by herself. This woman was ostracized by the rest of the town and rumored to be a lesbian. The little girl both wondered and feared if she would grow to be like her.

Martin maintains that discrimination prevents adults from being more open about their homosexuality, thus denying "suitable role models to gay adolescents who could demonstrate by example, sharing, and teaching that existing prejudices are false."[24] This is especially true for gay adults who work with children and adolescents.

Gender nonconformity may finally be a conscious effort to reject traditional roles and establish a separate and viable identity. One young lesbian told me she threw away her dolls in disgust when she was a child. It is not unusual for individuals sharing a common identity to separate themselves from others by establishing particular behaviors, appearances, terminology, and interests. Effeminacy in young gay males and masculinity in young lesbians is often a way for them to affirm a homosexual identity and assist them in finding each other. According to Wolf, culturally defined masculine attire is "more strongly assumed by young women who are newly aware of their lesbianism and looking for a community."[22]

Gay and lesbian youth take tremendous risks by being open about who they are. You have to respect their courage. They remain at high risk to suicidal feelings and behavior because of the pressures they face in conflicts with others about their homosexual orientation and the disappointments they experience at the initial hardships of an openly gay and lesbian lifestyle. Rofes warns that no myth is more dangerous to gay adolescents than the notion that "coming out" will insure them against feelings of self-destructiveness.[19]

The immediate conflicts that openly gay youth face are with their peers and family. Openly homosexual youth are an affront to a society that would like to believe they don't exist. Our culture seems to have particular disdain for those gay youth who do not conform to gender expectations. Rejection or abuse can become so intense that suicidal feelings and behavior result. Openly gay youth are more likely to be forced to leave their schools and families and survive on their own.

Those gay youth forced to become self-sufficient prematurely find that they face the discrimination of society against both youth and homosexuals in trying to do so. Often these youth have not had vocational training and some have not completed their secondary education. They are discriminated against in finding housing and employment because of their sexual orientation. Perhaps most disappointing, gay youth find they often cannot depend on help from adult gay males and lesbians in getting established because of the fears adult homosexuals have of being seen as "recruiting" young people. Gay youth often become involved with a small and unstable population of gay males and lesbians living on the streets. Here, they are at high risk at substance abuse, sexually transmitted diseases, and unstable relationships. The hardships of this lifestyle combined with the early rejection by family and peers may result in a suicide attempt.

> One young gay male involved in prostitution attempted suicide after receiving a "hate" letter from his parents. In it his mother said she was sorry she had not gotten an abortion before he was born and his father said that he only had half of a son. The young man completed suicide two years later.

A final area of difficulty for openly lesbian and gay male youth is in the forming and maintenance of intimate relationships with others. Having a lover is frequently a new experience for gay youth. Lewis writes:

> The lesbian's exploration of intimate experiences with other women is an emotionally turbulent process. It is, essentially, a second adolescence, complete with many of the symptoms common to the mainstream heterosexual adolescent period.[22]

The lack of experience that youth bring to these relationships is compounded by the need for secrecy and lack of social supports for dealing with conflicts so common in homosexual relationships. These first romantic involvements often assume a disproportionate importance in the youth's life. They serve to both affirm a lesbian or gay orientation and also fill unmet needs for love, caring, and friendship that have often been missing in the youth's life. When the relationship ends, gay youth sometimes feel no one cares and nothing is left to live for.

Ethnic Minority Gay Youth

Ethnic minority youth (i.e., Black, Hispanic, Asian, and American Indian) comprise a substantial number of youth who are gay, lesbian, bisexual, or transsexual. Ruth Hughes, Coordinator of Gay Youth Services at the Center for Special Problems in San Francisco, reports that these youth face more severe social and cultural oppression than other gay youth and far more serious problems than other adolescents.[29] Bell and Weinberg found that black gay males and lesbians attempted or seriously considered suicide at a rate less than white homosexuals but greater than black heterosexuals.[2] However, they found that a higher percentage of suicide attempts by black homosexuals took place during their youth. Thirty-six percent of black lesbians compared to 21 percent of white lesbians and 32 percent of black gay males compared to 27 percent of white gay males attempted suicide before age 18. This indicates that black gay youth may face particular hardships during adolescence.

Ethnic minority gay youth face all of the problems that other gay and lesbian youth face growing up in a hostile and condemning society. They also face the same economic discrimination and prejudice confronted by other ethnic minority youth because of racism. Davis notes a dramatic increase in suicides among young blacks over the past two decades that has brought their suicide rate nearly equal to that of white youths.[30] Hendin, in his book *Black Suicide,* offers an explanation:

> It does not seem surprising that suicide becomes a problem at such a relatively early age for the black person. A sense of despair, a feeling that life will never be satisfying confronts many blacks at a far younger age than it does most whites.[31]

Ethnic minority gay youth additionally face racial discrimination from white homosexuals that is a reflection of their treatment by the majority culture. Dutton writes that the gay liberation movement has often failed to consider the needs of ethnic minorities while ignoring their issues and concerns.[32] Jones adds that:

Little has been written about Third World sexual minorities, and when generalities were made about our lifestyles, attitudes, and behaviors, they were often made in reference to white cultures — white cultures being the basis for Third World cultures to deviate from or strive for.[33]

Finally, ethnic minority gay youth must contend with discrimination and special problems from their own ethnic group because of their sexual orientation. Hughes believes that ostracism and separation from their own ethnic group is particularly painful and difficult for these youth to cope with:

They expect acceptance by those like themselves who understand and have experienced oppression. Too often, blacks don't want to face the issue and see homosexuality as a struggle for white gay males. Ethnic minority gay youth are seen as an "embarrassment" to their cultural group. There is more concern for daily survival issues than an increased understanding of homosexuality.[29]

Jones adds that:

Lesbians and gays growing up in Third World communities experience just as much, if not more, oppression as heterosexual minority youth do in non–Third World communities. Unfortunately, most of the negative attitudes and oppressions bestowed upon lesbians and gays in Third World cultures are reactions to the influence that mainstream white culture has on it.[33]

Two issues that strongly affect ethnic minority gay youth are religion and the family.

Ethnic minority cultures have historically believed that homosexuality is a sin according to the faiths to which they predominantly belong. Parents frequently use religion as the standard to evaluate homosexuality. A homosexual orientation in their son or daughter becomes incompatible with religious beliefs. Ethnic minority gay youth often internalize these religious values and feel guilty for having homosexual feelings and experiences, fearing they are condemned to hell.

The family also plays a central role in the lives of these youth with strong expectations that they will fulfill social roles and perpetuate the extended family. A homosexual orientation is sometimes seen as a sign of disrespect to the family by the youth and a threat to the family's survival.

Ethnic minority gay youth have tremendous fears of losing their extended family and being alone in the world. This fear is made greater by the isolation they already face in our society as people of color. These ethnic minority gay youth who are rejected by families are at risk of suicide because of the tremendous pressures they face being gay and a person of color in a white homophobic society.

Transsexual Youth

Transsexual youth are perhaps the most outcast of all young people and face a grave risk of suicidal feelings and behavior. Huxdly and Brandon found that 53 percent of 72 transsexuals surveyed had made suicide attempts.[34] Harry feels that "transsexuals may be at higher risk than homosexuals and much higher risk than the general population" to suicidal behavior.[35] Transsexual youth believe they have a gender identity different from the sex they were born with. They often manifest this belief beginning in childhood through an expressed desire to be a person of the opposite gender, repudiation of their genitalia, gender nonconformity, and cross-dressing.[25] These behaviors may subside by adolescence due to extreme pressures to conform to social expectations. Some transsexual youth, however, try to "pass" in junior high and high school as a person of the opposite sex or engage in increasingly pronounced behaviors that do not conform to gender expectations. These adaptations present serious internal and external conflicts for these youth.

All transsexuals are vulnerable to internalizing an extremely negative image of themselves. They experience tremendous internal conflict between this image and their persistent desire to become the person they believe they are. Heller notes that suicidal transsexuals tend to feel hopelessly trapped in their situation.[36] These feelings may be particularly pronounced in young transsexuals who are forced to hide their identity. While wanting to change their sex, they are seldom able to do so and feel condemned to a life they are convinced is a mistake. The DSM III notes that transsexuals frequently experience "considerable anxiety and depression, which the individual may attribute to inability to live in the role of the desired sex."[25] This depression combined with a poor self-esteem can easily result in suicidal feelings and behavior in transsexual youth.

Some transsexual youth, however, make increasingly braver attempts to live as a person of the opposite sex. They experience conflicts in making a social adaptation to their believed identity. Many young transsexuals will adopt the most stereotyped roles and behaviors traditionally associated with being a "male" and a "female" in our society. Like other youth, they are trying to define themselves by rigid adherence to these roles. Sometimes transsexual youth experience problems similar to this:

> A young transsexual male was arrested for soliciting an undercover police officer while in drag. He was taken to juvenile hall where he experienced anxiety and confusion around his role in the unit with other boys. One time he reported it was his duty as the "only girl" to provide the other boys with sexual favors. Another time he broke down crying feeling as though he was being used and abused by the other males. A week later he made a suicide attempt.

Transsexual youth who are open about their identity face extreme abuse and rejection from families and peers. Many are forced to leave their home communities and survive on the streets. Their prognosis in our society is poor and they are at high risk of suicide. Gender dysphoria is a disorder that we have little understanding of and a great deal of repulsion for. The only known course of treatment is to help transsexuals to adjust to their believed gender identity and obtain sex-reassignment surgery. Most transsexual youth, however, are unable to obtain or afford the help they need in resolving their identity conflicts.

It is important to distinguish between transsexual youth and gay and lesbian youth who do not conform to gender expectations. Gender nonconformity is common among gay youth in both childhood and adolescence. Some gay and lesbian youth may experience gender identity confusion during adolescence in the coming-out process because of the intense social pressures for gay males to be like women and lesbians to be like men. Gay youth may feel they actually have to be a person of the opposite gender to meet those expectations. Hughes, in her work with both homosexual and transsexual youth, emphasizes the importance of working with a young person over a period of time to determine if they are truly a transsexual.[29] Gay and lesbian youth come to recognize that they neither want to change their sex nor live as a person of the opposite gender.

RISK FACTORS IN GAY AND LESBIAN YOUTH SUICIDE

Gay young people face the same risk factors for suicidal behavior that affect other youth. These include family problems, breaking up with a lover, social isolation, school failure, and identity conflicts. However, these factors assume greater importance when the youth has a gay or lesbian orientation. Jay and Young found that 53 percent of gay males and 33 percent of lesbians surveyed believed their suicide attempts involved their homosexuality.[1] Bell and Weinberg report that 58 percent of gay males and 39 percent of lesbians felt their first suicide attempts were related to the fact that they were homosexuals.[2] Suicide attempts by gay and lesbian youth are even more likely to involve conflicts around their sexual orientation because of the overwhelming pressures they face in coming out at an early age.

General

Bell and Weinberg found that initial suicide attempts related to homosexuality more frequently involved acceptance of self and conflicts with others for gay males, while lesbians tended to cite problems with lovers as the reason.[2] Self-acceptance may be especially critical for young gay males, who tend to have homosexual experiences and are aware of their orientation at a somewhat earlier age than lesbians.[1,15] Conflicts with others may be more salient for young gay males identified as homosexuals. Gender nonconformity elicits a negative response from others for lesbian and gay male youth, but society seems to have particular disdain for effeminate young males. Young lesbians may experience more extreme social isolation, often reporting an absence of same-sex experiences or knowing others like them during adolescence. They also face stronger social pressures to fulfill the woman's traditional role of marrying and having children and may experience more depression related to not meeting social expectations. Problems with lovers may be especially critical for young lesbians because their sexuality is often explored within the context of their early intimate relationships.

The earlier a youth is aware of a gay or lesbian orientation, the greater the problems they face and more likely the risk of suicidal feelings and behavior. Remafedi observes that:

> Younger gay adolescents may be at the highest risk for dysfunction because of emotional and physical immaturity, unfulfilled developmental needs for identification with a peer group, lack of experience, and dependence on parents unwilling or unable to provide emotional support.[5]

He adds that younger gay adolescents are more likely to abuse substances, drop out of school, be in conflict with the law, undergo psychiatric hospitalization, run away from home, be involved in prostitution, and attempt suicide. The Los Angeles Suicide Prevention Center recently found that the strongest causative indicators of suicidal behavior among gay youth were awareness of their sexual orientation, depression and suicidal feelings, and substance abuse — all before age 14.[7] A 14-year-old gay male interviewed for this paper confirms that profile:

> When I was 11, I started smoking dope, drinking alcohol, and snorting speed every day to make me feel better and forget I was gay. I would party with friends but get more and more depressed as the night would go on. They would always make antigay remarks and harass gay men while I would just stand there. Late at night, after they went home, I would go down to the river and dive in — hoping I would hit my head on a rock and drown.[23]

Society

It is a sobering fact to realize that we are the greatest risk factor in gay youth suicide. No group of people are more strongly affected by the attitudes and conduct of society than are the young. Gay and lesbian youth are strongly affected by the negative attitudes and hostile responses of society to homosexuality. The resulting poor self-esteem, depression, and fear can be a fatal blow to a fragile identity. Two ways that society influences suicidal behavior by gay and lesbian youth are: (1) the ongoing discrimination against and oppression of homosexuals, and (2) the portrayal of homosexuals as being self-destructive.

It is the response of our society as a whole to homosexuality, and specifically those institutions and significant others responsible for their care, that pose the greatest risk to gay and lesbian youth. Gock believes that homophobia, the irrational fear and hatred of homosexuals, is the root of the problem.[37] Gay males and lesbians are still routinely the victims of violence by others. In a recent survey of nearly 2,100 lesbians and gay men nationwide, the National Gay Task Force found that more than 90 percent had been victims of verbal and physical assault because of their sexual orientation.[10] Tacit and explicit discrimination against homosexuals is still pervasive in virtually all areas of life. Half of the States still prohibit homosexual relationships between consenting adults.[37] Homosexuals are not allowed to legally marry and form "legitimate" long-term relationships. The vast majority of States and municipalities still discriminate against lesbians and gay men in housing, employment, and other areas. Gay and lesbian youth see this and take it to heart.

Rofes warns us against the myth that homosexuality, in and of itself, encourages suicide.[13] There is nothing inherently self-destructive in homosexual feelings and relationships that could be a source of suicidal behavior. In his book *I Thought People Like That Killed Themselves*, Rofes maintains we have created a stereotyped image of the unhappy homosexual in literature and the media (e.g., *Boys in the Band)* for which suicide is the only appropriate resolution. This image is reinforced by the fact that homosexual characters in novels and films invariably kill themselves in the end. The myth is perpetuated by the absence of positive adult gay role models in our society, where, historically, the only known homosexuals were those exposed by scandal and disgraced in their communities. Rofes maintains this creates a strong negative context for the early identity formation of young gay males and lesbians, effectively socializing them into suicidal feelings and behavior. He sees a strong correlation between sexual orientation, social response to that sexual orientation, and subsequent suicidality in an individual.

Self-Esteem

A predisposing factor in suicidal feelings among many adolescents is poor self-esteem. This is especially true for gay adolescents who have internalized a harshly negative image of being bad and wrong from society, religion, family, and peers. For youth, a poor self-image contributes substantially to a lack of confidence in being able to cope with problems. The images of homosexuals as sick and self-destructive have impact on the coping skills of gay youth, rendering them helpless and unable to improve their situation. Gay youth who have internalized a message throughout their lives of being worthless and unable to cope from abusive and chaotic families are at even greater risk.

Youth with a poor self-esteem and poor coping skills are particularly vulnerable to suicidal feelings when confronting a problem for the first time. They really don't know how to resolve it or even if they can. Gay youth are highly susceptible to suicidal feelings during the "coming-out" process when first facing their own homosexuality and the hostile response it evokes in others. They may attempt suicide when they first realize they have homosexual feelings or a gay orientation. Some youth deny their homosexual feelings and engage in unconscious self-destructive behavior out of self-hatred. Others try to "change" their orientation and make a suicide attempt when they recognize their homosexuality will not go away and is part of who they are.

Many youth realize they are gay or lesbian but attempt to hide their orientation from others. They suffer from chronic loneliness and depression. They may attempt suicide because they feel trapped in their situation and believe they do not deserve to live. A suicidal gesture may be a cry for help from these youth for others to recognize and understand their situation. Finally, those youth who are open about being gay, lesbian, or bisexual face continuous conflict with their environment. They remain vulnerable to suicide because they face these extreme pressures with a more fragile sense of self-worth and ability to cope with life than other youth.

Family

Family problems are probably the most significant factor in youth suicide. Youth derive their core sense of being cared about and belonging from their families. Gay youth may make suicide attempts after being rejected by their families. For gay and lesbian youth forced to leave home, the loss of parental love and support remains a critical issue for them. Sometimes the youth's sexual orientation becomes a convenient excuse for parents to reject a son or daughter they did not want. Youth from abusive and dysfunctional families are at even greater risk. Wandrei found, in comparing suicide attempts by lesbians and heterosexual women, that [the] lesbians were more likely to come from broken homes.[39]

Gay and lesbian youth face more verbal and physical abuse from family members than do other youth. The National Gay Task Force found that more than 33 percent of gay males and lesbians reported verbal abuse from relatives because of their orientation and 7 percent reported physical abuse as well.[10] These figures are substantially higher for youth open about their sexual orientation while still living at home. Sometimes this harassment becomes too much to bear for gay youth and a suicide attempt results.

Gay and lesbian youth may feel suicidal because of a failure to meet family expectations. All youth need approval from their parents. Some youth report only feeling loved by parents when they are fulfilling their parents' image of who they should be. Gay youth often feel they cannot meet their parents' standards and may attempt suicide over real or anticipated disappointment by their families that they will not fit the social script of heterosexual marriage and grandchildren. This pressure is particularly strong for lesbians. Gay youth fear they will not have families of their own and be alone as adults with no one to care for them.

Communication problems also play a serious role in family issues for gay youth. Many lesbian and gay youth hide their orientation from their parents out of fear of rejection. They have often seen a strong negative reaction to homosexuality by parents and siblings, including homophobic remarks. The anticipated inevitable loss of love can precipitate a suicide attempt. Parris related a call to a suicide hotline in Washington, D.C.:

> The youth said that he was gay and wanted to talk with his parents about it but was afraid because they were very religious. A week later, a man called ... to say his son had committed suicide. They were

calling an unfamiliar number on their long-distance phone bill. By matching the man's address ... the tragic connection was made.[19]

Religion

Religion presents another risk factor in gay youth suicide because of the depiction of homosexuality as a sin and the reliance of families on the church for understanding homosexuality. Many traditional (e.g., Catholicism) and fundamentalist (e.g., Baptist) faiths still portray homosexuality as morally wrong or evil. Family religious beliefs can be a primary reason for parents forcing youth to leave home if a homosexual orientation is seen as incompatible with church teachings. These beliefs can also create unresolvable internal conflicts for gay youth who adhere to their faith but believe they will not change their sexual orientation. They may feel wicked and condemned to hell and attempt suicide in despair of ever obtaining redemption.

School

Many gay and lesbian youth feel trapped in school settings because of a compulsory obligation to attend and the inability to defend themselves against verbal and physical assaults. Schools do not adequately protect gay youth, with teachers often reluctant to stop harassment or rebut homophobic remarks for fear of being seen as undesirable role models.[19] Verbal and physical attacks against gay youth have increased in recent years as students become increasingly threatened by the presence and openness of peers with a lesbian or gay orientation. This abuse begins as early as late elementary school, becomes pronounced in junior high when youth are still immature, and continues into high school. The failure of schools to address this concern can be tragic:

> In Lebanon, Pennsylvania, in 1977, a 16-year-old boy fatally shot himself before entering the 10th grade. He left a suicide note explaining he could not return to school and sustain the abuse and ridicule about being gay from his classmates. A few friends at school supported [him] though they knew he was gay, but the majority ridiculed him without mercy. He skipped classes to avoid the torture and welcomed the summer vacation as a respite. But he was already taking pills to escape the reality of the approach of another school term, when

he would have to move from junior high to the even more sharply defined roles of senior high. On September 3 he shared that anxiety with a friend and on September 5 he shot and killed himself.[40]

The failure of schools to educate youth about homosexuality presents another risk factor to gay and lesbian adolescents. By ignoring the subject in all curricula, including family life classes, the schools deny access to positive information about homosexuality that could improve the self-esteem of gay youth. They also perpetuate myths and stereotypes that condemn homosexuality and deny youth access to positive adult lesbian and gay role models. This silence provides tacit support for homophobic attitudes and conduct by some students.

Social Isolation

Social isolation has been consistently identified as one of the most critical factors in suicide attempts by youth. The isolation and alienation young people experience in all aspects of their lives can be overwhelming. Those youth hiding their identity often withdraw from family and friends out of fear of being discovered. They feel there is no one they can talk to and no one who will understand. Tartagni, based on his experience teaching in public school, writes that "one of the loneliest people in any high school in America is the rejected and isolated gay adolescent."[41] This isolation may be more extreme for young lesbians, who often report a total lack of contact with others like themselves during high school. Joanne, in *One Teenager in Ten,* describes her feelings after realizing her lesbianism in adolescence:

> In October, I realized my lesbianism and I did not have someone gay to talk with. I recall the anguish I suffered looking back over my journal during that time period. "Please. Help me. Oh shit, I have to talk with someone ... I have to tell someone, ask someone. WHO??!! Dammit all, would someone please help me? Someone, anyone. Help me. I'm going to kill myself if they don't."[28]

Openly gay youth experience blatant rejection and isolation from others. One young gay male related that his parents refused to eat at the dinner table with him after they learned he was gay. Male peers cruelly separate themselves from young gay males with jokes about not wanting to get AIDS. Gay youth frequently do not have contact with other gay adolescents or adults for support. Parents often forbid them from associating with people they "suspect" or know to be homosexuals. Youth service workers often feel uncomfortable talking with gay young people because of their prejudices and lack of understanding for who they are. The Los Angeles Suicide Prevention Center, in their recent study on gay youth suicide, ironically found that gay young people rated social support as being very important to them while simultaneously experiencing people as being more rejecting of them than did other youth.[7]

Substance Abuse

Some gay and lesbian young people cope with the many problems they face by using alcohol and drugs. The age of onset for substance use among all youth has become lower in recent years and in 1985 is estimated to be 11.9 years for boys and 12.7 years for girls.[42] This coincides with the age that many youth are becoming aware of a gay or lesbian orientation. Rofes found that lesbians and gay men have a higher rate of substance abuse than heterosexuals and found this to be correlated with increased suicidal feelings and behavior.[13]

Gay youth are especially susceptible to substance abuse in trying to cope with the conflicts of the coming-out process. Remafedi believes there may be a higher rate of substance abuse among gay youth than among gay adults.[5] He found that 58 percent of young gay males he interviewed could be classified as having a substance abuse disorder in the DSM III. Gay youth forced to live on the streets experience more severe drug problems. The Larkin Street Youth Center in San Francisco reported that more than 75 percent of their clients identified as gay had serious and chronic disorders.[8] The Los Angeles Suicide Prevention Center found a strong correlation between substance abuse and suicide attempts among gay young people.[7]

Professional Help

Perhaps no risk factor is as insidious or unique to the suicidal behavior of gay and lesbian youth than receiving professional help. The large number of gay youth who have had contact with mental health and social work services during their turbulent adolescent years would seem to be a positive indicator for improving their stability and future outlook. This is sadly not often the case. Many helping professionals still refuse to recognize or accept a homosexual orientation in youth despite growing evidence that sexual orientation is formed by adolescence.[15] They refuse to support a homosexual orientation in youth despite the fact that homosexuality is no longer viewed as a mental disorder.[25] They continue to insist that homosexual feelings are just a passing "phase," while making the goal of treatment arresting or changing those feelings and experiences. Martin pointedly describes this process:

> Pain and suffering are inflicted on the very young, whom society is supposedly protecting, under the guise of preventing the spread of homosexuality or of treating the individual.[24]

He adds that some psychiatrists even advocate creating conflict, guilt, and anxiety in adolescents concerned about homosexual feelings where none has previously existed.

Youth who deny their feelings and experience "ego-dystonic homosexuality" are especially vulnerable to this type of adverse treatment. Rather than helping these youth to accept and understand predominantly homosexual feelings and experiences, we see their denial as a "hopeful" sign that they can still develop a heterosexual orientation. When homosexual feelings persist after treatment has attempted to change them, the youth despairs and is at potentially greater risk for suicide than if we tried to help him/her toward acceptance.

Youth who are aware of their lesbian or gay orientation but hide it from others may seek help without identifying their concerns about their sexuality. We often do not recognize these youth because we don't acknowledge they exist. We are uncomfortable in discussing or addressing the issue and consequently are unable to identify or resolve the source of the youth's conflicts. A suicide attempt may be an effort by the youth to force the issue and bring it to our attention. It may also be an act of despair over a problem that they feel cannot be addressed through professional help.

Even openly gay and lesbian youth are subjected to treatment with potentially adverse effects. Frequently, informing family and counselors that a youth is gay is the impetus for imposed treatment. We assume that the youth's gay orientation is the source of the problem rather than the response of others to his/her being lesbian or gay.

Encouraging these youth to change can cause regression in the development of a healthy gay identity and reinforce traditional stereotypes of homosexuals as sick and self-destructive. This, in turn, further weakens the youth's self-esteem and ability to cope with problems. Even those professionals who accept the youth as gay or lesbian are often unable to support the youngster in dealing with conflicts at home and in school.

Youth Programs

There is a critical lack of program resources for gay and lesbian youth. Many social and recreational programs for youth make no effort to incorporate gay young people into their services. Few programs will accept or support a gay adolescent in their sexual orientation. Agency policies tacitly or explicitly forbid the hiring of openly gay and lesbian staff, denying gay youth access to positive adult gay role models. Homophobic remarks and attitudes by youth and staff in many of these programs go unrebutted. Consequently, gay youth do not use many of the youth service resources available to them or soon leave if they do. This increases their social isolation and alienation from their peers.

Other gay and lesbian youth who are wards of the juvenile court have little choice but to live in those placements to which they are referred. Here, they re-experience many of the problems they had in their home communities. Many foster families are rejecting of gay and lesbian youth, feeling less investment than a youth's natural family to keeping the youth in the home. Gay male and lesbian adults are prohibited in most States from being foster parents, with gay youth again denied access to supportive adults who could serve as positive role models for them.

Group home placements present special hardships for gay youth because abusive peers often live in the same home with them. Those programs without an on-site school require gay youth to return to public school for their education. Program staff have seldom received training on issues and concerns related to homosexuality. They are frequently unable to understand or work with gay youth effectively. Group homes become a living hell of harassment, isolation, and conflict, with other staff and residents offering gay youth little support and no resolution. A suicide attempt may be an effort to force removal from the placement and find a different home. Many homes, however, will not accept gay youth, and few offer specialized services to meet their needs.

Relationships with Lovers

We are all victims of the myth that our first love will be our one true love until death do us part (e.g., Romeo and Juliet). Young people are especially vulnerable to this misconception, and breaking up with a lover is one of the most frequent reasons for their suicide attempts. The first romantic involvements of lesbian and gay male youth are a source of great joy to them in affirming their sexual identity, providing them with support, and assuring them that they too can experience love. However, society places extreme hardships on these relationships that make them difficult to establish and maintain. Bell and Weinberg found that relationship problems were the single most frequently cited reason for the initial suicide attempts of lesbians (62%) and gay males (42%).[2]

Intimate relationships are the primary focus of hostility and discrimination against homosexuals. Society severely restricts where homosexuals can meet, prevents public displays of affection between them, and does not allow legal marriages to be formed. Gay and lesbian youth suffer greater isolation than homosexual adults and far greater social deprivation than other adolescents. It is extremely difficult for them to meet other homosexuals, and they frequently do not know anyone like themselves. Gay youth who hide their identity often form their first romantic attachments to unknowing friends, teachers, and peers. These are often cases of unrequited love, with the youth never revealing their true feelings. Gay youth are fragile in these situations and may experience despair or suicidal feelings from never being able to fulfill their hopes for a relationship. Some gay youth bravely reveal their feelings and may attempt suicide after blatant rejection by a teacher or the loss of a close friend.

Young gay males often experience their first homosexual relationships as brief sexual encounters in clandestine meeting places (e.g., parks). The extreme need for secrecy and anonymous nature of these contacts seriously hinder their further development. The intensity of sexual feelings that accompany these encounters can easily be mistaken for romantic attachment by young gay males. They may feel suicidal at the failure of these experiences to meet intimacy needs and the inability to fulfill the social expectation of sustaining the relationship. Young lesbians experience greater isolation than young males. They are less likely to explore their sexuality or have relationships during adolescence. They may feel suicidal at the despair of ever finding love in relationships with other women.

Gay and lesbian youth develop intimate relationships at a later age than other youth and are unable to develop relationship skills in the manner of other adolescents. Their first romances are an emotionally turbulent trial-and-error process that resembles a second adolescence. Gay youth bring to these relationships extreme dependency needs resulting from the deprivation experienced in their relationships with family and peers. They also are still in the process of forming their identity and have unresolved issues of guilt and poor self-esteem. When conflicts arise in homosexual relationships, there are few social supports available to assist them. This is compounded for gay youth by their frequent need for secrecy and the fact that they may not be open about their identity with family and friends.

Breaking up with a lover may confirm earlier negative experiences and concepts associated with being a homosexual. Young lesbians often explore and define their sexuality within the context of their first relationships. A relationship failure for them may be synonymous with problems in developing a positive lesbian identity. For some gay youth, relationships become a way of filling needs for love and belonging missing from family and peers. When the relationship ends, the youth feel as though they have lost everything. They fear that they will always be alone, that no one cares, and nothing is worth living for.

Independent Living

Gay and lesbian youth are more likely than other adolescents to be forced to leave home and become self-sufficient prematurely. Some of these youth have been hiding their identities and can no longer stand the extreme isolation in their lives. Many others have been rejected by families and have dropped out of school, effectively forced out of their communities because of their sexual orientation. Gay youth come to large cities hoping to find others like themselves, legitimate employment, a lover, and a new "family." They soon become aware of the lack of opportunities available to them and become enmeshed in the problem of survival. Suicidal feelings emerge as the hope for a new and better life begins to pale.

Most gay youth are unprepared for the difficulties they encounter. They are discriminated against in finding employment and housing by virtue of being both young and homosexual. Many have no vocational training and some were not able to finish high school. They often find limited support from the lesbian and gay male adult community, who fear involvement with youth. Many are forced to turn to the streets for survival. A recent study on adolescent male prostitution found that nearly 75 percent identified themselves as gay or bisexual, with family conflicts as the primary reason for leaving home.[43] Many gay youth become homeless. Others depend on relationships with people they meet on the streets to obtain shelter and survival needs.

Gay youth living on the streets are at greater risk of suicide due to repeated exposure to chronic substance abuse, physical and sexual assault, and sexually transmitted diseases, including AIDS. Their contact with the limited segment of gay adults involved in street life confirms a negative image of homosexuality, and they remain unaware of the variety of positive adult gay lifestyles open to them. Their relationships are tenuous and complicated by dependence on their lovers for support. Some gay and lesbian youth engage in increasingly reckless and self-destructive behavior as an expression of the sadness and anger they feel because of the unresolved issues with their families and despair over their new life. A suicide attempt may result from a negative contact with their family, breaking up with a lover, or failure to make it on their own.

AIDS (Acquired Immune Deficiency Syndrome)

Gay and bisexual male youth again belong to two groups at high risk of contracting sexually transmitted diseases: gay/bisexual males and adolescents. Although the number of confirmed cases of AIDS and ARCs (AIDS Related Conditions) among adolescents is small, it is believed that cumulative exposure to the virus, beginning in adolescence, may result in a diagnosis or symptoms as a young adult. Gay and bisexual males have always been subject to a greater number of health problems through sexually transmitted diseases (STDs). They comprise a substantial majority of confirmed cases of AIDS, and more than 50 percent of adult gay males will contract Hepatitis Type B during their lifetime.[44]

Young people are taught in our society that sex is a secretive and spontaneous activity. Adolescent males are not encouraged to take responsibility for their sexual behavior; the vast majority do not take precautions in their sex practices. They engage in impulsive and unplanned sexual activity with grave consequences. Young people contract several million cases of STDs every year.[45] Gay and bisexual male youth are particularly vulnerable because of their need for secrecy in sexual contacts and the frequency with which they engage in unplanned sexual activity. Those gay and bisexual male youth living on the streets face a substantially greater risk of exposure to STDs because of repeated sexual contacts in their relationships and prostitution experiences. Street youth face additional exposure through intravenous drug use.

Sexual experiences are important to gay male youth as a way of exploring and affirming their sexual orientation. Many do not take precautions and share a feeling of invulnerability to future conse- quences that is common among all youth. Remafedi found, however, that 45 percent of young gay males interviewed had a history of STDs.[5] The attitudes of young gay males toward exposure to AIDS ranges from denial to extreme fear to not caring. One young male said he was not concerned because "teenagers do not get AIDS." Another was convinced that a head cold he had developed was the first symp- tom of AIDS. Those who are at greatest risk may be those who simply do not care whether they are exposed to the virus. Some gay youth have an uncaring approach to life that reflects a "suicidal script." They are more prone to self-destructive behavior because of the severity of the problems they have experienced throughout their lives and specifi- cally in relation to their sexual orientation. Contracting AIDS becomes for them the fulfillment of a life of pain and suffering they no longer want to cope with. They feel that they deserve to die.

Future Outlook

A final risk factor for gay and lesbian youth suicide is a bleak outlook for the future. Young people have difficulty seeing a future life that is different from the present. Gay and lesbian youth fear their lives will always be as unhappy and hard as they presently are. They do not know that they will receive any more caring, acceptance, and support than they are getting now. The little information they have about homosexuality usually reinforces these mistaken beliefs. Gay youth do not understand what life could be like as a gay male or lesbian adult. They do not have accurate information about homosexuality, positive role models to pattern themselves after, or knowledge of gay and lesbian adult lifestyles and communities. Lesbian and gay youth frequently don't know that many lesbian and gay male adults lead stable, happy, and productive lives. They go through adolescence feeling lonely, afraid, and hopeless. Sometimes they take their own lives.

ENDING GAY AND LESBIAN YOUTH SUICIDE

We can substantially reduce the risk of suicide among gay and lesbian youth. The problem is clearly one of providing information, acceptance, and support to gay youth for coping with the pressures and conflicts they face growing up as homosexuals in our society. However, in addressing their concerns, we confront two issues of greater magnitude: (1) the discrimination against and maltreatment of homosexuals by our society and (2) the inability of our society to recognize or accept the existence of homosexuality in the young. The homophobia experienced by gay youth in all parts of their lives is the primary reason for their suicidal feelings and behavior. Rofes notes that it is no longer difficult to document the violence, shame, and hatred by society with which lesbians and gay men have lived.[13] This is the issue we must address to save the lives of gay males and lesbians who are young.

Society

The first step in ending gay youth suicide is to end the discrimination against and stigmatization of homosexuals in our society. We have tenaciously clung to lies and prejudices about homosexuals for far too long. Too many lives have been brutalized and lost. A growing body of research contradicts our negative biases and assumptions about gay males and lesbians. We do not, as a society, want to continue to hold the untenable position of senselessly hurting others — especially the young. Gay males and lesbians need to be accepted as equal partners in our society. Laws should safeguard their individual rights and not permit discrimination against them in housing, employment, and other areas. Laws prohibiting homosexual relationships between consenting adults should be repealed and marriages between homosexuals should be recognized. Special attention should be paid to the enforcement of laws that punish those who commit violence against homosexuals. Laws can help to establish the principle of equality for lesbians and gay men and define the conduct of others in their interactions with them.

It is an even more comprehensive task to address the negative attitudes about homosexuality held by so many people. A conscious effort must be made to dispel the destructive myths about homosexuality at all levels of society. We must promote a positive image of gay males and lesbians to reduce oppression against them and provide gay youth with role models to pattern themselves after. Massive education efforts need to take place that would provide people with accurate information about homosexuality. These efforts especially need to be directed to those who have responsibility for the care of the young including families, clergy, teachers, and helping professionals. The media needs to take responsibility for promoting a positive image of homosexuals that presents a variety of gay male and lesbian lifestyles. We must also take personal responsibility for revising our own homophobic attitudes and behavior as an example to others in the same way that we have worked toward revising discriminatory racial attitudes and conduct. It is at the personal level that we have the greatest impact on the lives of those around us.

Third, we must directly address the issue of homosexuality in the young. Our society has historically denied the sexuality of young people. We must educate ourselves on the issues and problems related to sexual development in young people. Society needs to promote a positive image about sexuality and provide youth with accurate information on the subject. We need to recognize that youth are sexually active from an early age and that sexual orientation is frequently formed by adolescence. All youth need to be provided with positive information about homosexuality that presents it as a viable adaptation. We must accept a homosexual orientation in young people in the same manner we accept a heterosexual orientation. Finally, we need to assist gay and lesbian young people in the coming-out process and support them in the many conflicts they presently face.

Family

Gay and lesbian youth need to receive acceptance and under-standing from their families if we are to reduce their risk of suicide. Parents need to be educated as to the nature and development of homosexuality in individuals. They often feel guilty and ashamed upon first learning that their child is gay because they have been told that it is wrong and they are to blame. Parents should know that homosexuality is a natural and healthy form of sexual expression. They do not need to feel bad about something that is good. Parents should also know that we still do not know the origins of a heterosex-ual or homosexual orientation. Research indicates a predisposition toward sexual orientation in children that limits the role of family in its development.

Families have a great deal of influence on how their children feel about their sexual orientation. Parents should be made aware of the potential negative impact homophobic remarks and behavior have on their child. Homophobic conduct can be taken as rejection by youth struggling with their sexual orientation or encouragement by other youth to victimize homosexuals as they grow older. Families need to take responsibility for presenting homosexuality in a positive context to their children. Parents need to accept and understand a son or daughter with a homosexual orientation. Those parents who have difficulty accepting their lesbian daughter or gay son should get more information on the subject and not try to "change" them. They should let the child know they are still loved and cared about as individuals regardless of their sexual orientation.

Ethnic minority families need to understand and accept their gay and lesbian children. Ethnic minority youth depend even more strongly on their extended family and culture for support because of the additional oppression they face as a racial minority within society as a whole and the homosexual community. Parents need to be edu-cated as to the extent and diversity of lesbians and gay males within ethnic minority cultures. They need to understand that their child means no disrespect to the family and cannot be any different from who they are.

Society needs to reinforce parental responsibility for the care of their child, irrespective of sexual orientation, until they become adults. Parents need to be held accountable for the abuse of their children related to their homosexual orientation. We need to become more conscious of the extent to which the abuse of gay adolescents occurs within their own families.

Religion

Religions need to reassess homosexuality in a positive context within their belief systems. They need to accept gay youth and make a place for them in the church and include them in the same activities as other youth. Religions should also take responsibility for providing their families and membership with positive information about homosexuality that discourages the oppression of lesbians and gay men. Faiths that condemn homosexuality should recognize how they contribute to the rejection of gay youth by their families and suicide among lesbian and gay male youth.

Schools

Public and private schools need to take responsibility for providing all students at the junior high and high school level with positive information about homosexuality. Curriculum materials should include information relevant to gay males and lesbians as it pertains to human sexuality, health, literature, and social studies. Family life classes should present homosexuality as a natural and healthy form of sexual expression. Information on critical health issues such as AIDS should be presented to all students. Curricula should include values clarification around social roles to increase the respect for individual differences and reduce the stigma attached to gender nonconformity. A variety of gay male and lesbian adult lifestyles should be presented as positive and viable for youth. All youth should learn about prominent lesbians and gay males throughout history. Social studies courses should include issues relevant to gay male and lesbian concerns and provide youth with positive gay and lesbian adult role models in our society.

Schools need to take responsibility for protecting gay and lesbian youth from abuse by peers and providing them with a safe environment to receive an education. School staff need to receive training on how to work with gay youth and handle conflicts involving gay youth. Teachers should feel secure in being able to rebut homophobic remarks and defend gay youth against harassment. Strong disciplinary actions should be imposed on those who victimize gay and lesbian youth. It is important for schools to hire openly gay male and lesbian teachers to serve as role models and resource people for gay youth. Counseling services that are sensitive to the needs and concerns of gay youth should be available to them. Special educational programs may need to be developed for those youth who cannot be incorporated into existing school settings to ensure that young gay males and lesbians receive an equal education.

Social Support

Gay and lesbian youth need access to the same social supports and recreational activities that other youth have. This would reduce their isolation and enhance their positive social development. Communities need to develop social groups and activities (i.e., dances) specifically for gay and lesbian youth as a way of meeting others like themselves and developing relationship skills. Existing youth programs such as the Boy and Girl Scouts should incorporate gay youth into their activities. Youth programs such as Big Brothers and Sisters should enlist gay and lesbian adults to work with gay youth. It is very important for gay youth to see the potential of a happy and stable lifestyle as adults. Lesbians and gay men need to become more involved in supporting gay youth and being positive role models for them. This requires assurance for gay adults that they will not be harassed and accused of "recruiting" youth in doing so.

Professional Help

Lesbian and gay youth must have access to social services and professional counseling that is sensitive to their needs and able to address their concerns. This is critical to reducing their risk of suicide. Sexuality is one of the most important issues facing all young people. We need to be open about sexuality and accepting of homosexuality in young people. All social service agencies and mental health professionals working with youth need specialized training on homosexuality and issues relevant to gay and lesbian youth. We also need to address issues of suicide and depression in young people. Suicidality needs to be explored with youth who have a gay, lesbian, bisexual, or transsexual identity. Problems related to a homosexual orientation should be assessed as a possible reason for suicidal feelings. The goal of treatment should be to assist lesbian and gay youth in developing a positive identity and to support their sexual orientation in the conflicts they face with others. Additional counseling guidelines are provided in Appendix B.

Youth agencies need to provide outreach to gay and lesbian youth to make them aware of services and assure them that they are welcome. Gay youth are often afraid to seek help because of potential negative reactions from others. Programs should hire gay staff that reflect the population of gay youth under their care. Helping professionals should be prepared to offer referrals to gay-identified services and therapists if requested by the youth. It is an accepted premise in social services that individuals have access to programs and staff that reflect their cultural background. This principle is no less true for gay young people who often would prefer to talk about their problems with a lesbian or [a] gay man.

Specialized services should be developed for gay and lesbian youth that reflect their particular needs. Health care programs aimed at preventing AIDS and other sexually transmitted diseases need to be directed toward young gay males. Alcohol and substance abuse programs need to target gay and lesbian youth as a population at risk. Pregnancy-related services should not assume a heterosexual orientation in young women and be prepared to discuss lesbian concerns. Vocational training and independent-living skills programs may need to address special problems gay youth face in becoming self-sufficient and in being incorporated into an adult gay community.

Residential Programs

The juvenile justice system needs to take responsibility for ensuring that gay and lesbian youth receive fair treatment by the juvenile court and are placed in safe, nurturing, and supportive environments. Specialized training in working with and understanding gay youth should be provided to foster parents, group home personnel, treatment center staff, and juvenile hall counselors. Gay youth should be incorporated into placements, whenever possible, where the staff has been taught how to support gays in issues with other residents. It is critical for the juvenile court to show leadership in preventing discrimination against gay youth by prohibiting placements that refuse to accept them or that provide them with inferior care. The needs of some gay and

lesbian youth might best be served in the immediate future by placement in gay-identified foster or group homes. Extremely few such
placements presently exist. The juvenile court should facilitate the
licensing of gay male and lesbian foster parents along with the development of residential programs specifically for those gay youth who
cannot be incorporated into existing placements.

Research

The lack of information about gay and lesbian youth suicide is a
reflection of the oppression of homosexuals by our society and the
invisibility of large numbers of gay males and lesbians within the
youth population. There is growing awareness that a serious problem
exists, but we have only started to break down the wall of silence
surrounding the issue. Comprehensive research is needed to determine
the extent and nature of suicide among young gay males, lesbians,
bisexuals, and transsexuals. These studies need to ensure that the
entire spectrum of gay youth is adequately represented, including
lesbians, homeless youth, and ethnic minorities. This research can be
the foundation for greater recognition of the problem and the allocation of resources designed to address it. Hopefully, the work done in
recent years will serve as the beginning of the end of suicide among
gay and lesbian youth.

APPENDIX A:
RISK FACTORS IN GAY AND LESBIAN YOUTH SUICIDE

General
Awareness/identification of homosexual orientation at an early age
Self-acceptance of homosexual orientation
Conflicts with others related to homosexual orientation
Problems in homosexual relationships

Society
Discrimination/oppression of homosexuals by society
Portrayal of homosexuals as self-destructive by society

Poor Self-Esteem
Internalization of image of homosexuals as sick and bad
Internalization of image of homosexuals as helpless and self-destructive

Identity Conflicts
Denial of a homosexual orientation
Despair in recognition of a homosexual orientation

Family
Rejection of child due to homosexual orientation
Abuse/harassment of child due to homosexual orientation
Failure of child to meet parental/social expectation
Perceived rejection of child due to homosexual orientation

Religion
Child's homosexual orientation seen as incompatible with family religious beliefs
Youth feels sinful, condemned to hell due to homosexual orientation

School
Abuse/harassment of homosexual youth by peers
Lack of accurate information about homosexuality

Social Isolation
Rejection of homosexual youth by friends and peers
Social withdrawal of homosexual youth
Loneliness and inability to meet others like themselves

Substance Abuse
Substance use to relieve pain of oppression
Substance use to reduce inhibitions on homosexual feelings

Professional Help
  Refusal to accept homosexual orientation of youth
  Refusal to support homosexual orientation of youth
  Involuntary treatment to change homosexual orientation of youth
  Inability to discuss issues related to homosexuality

Residential Programs
  Refusal to accept/support homosexual orientation of youth
  Isolation of homosexual youth by staff and residents
  Inability to support homosexual youth in conflicts with residents

Relationship Problems
  Inability to develop relationship skills like heterosexual youth
  Extreme dependency needs due to prior emotional deprivation
  Absence of social supports in resolving relationship conflicts

Independent Living
  Lack of support from family
  Lack of support from adult gay community
  Involvement with street life

AIDS (Acquired Immune Deficiency Syndrome)
  Unsafe sexual practices
  Secrecy/unplanned nature of early sexual experiences

Future Outlook
  Despair of life as hard as the present
  Absence of positive adult gay/lesbian role models

APPENDIX B:
COUNSELING GAY AND LESBIAN YOUTH

Those of us who work with young people need to be able to identify gay and lesbian youth, accept them for who they are, and support them in resolving their problems. Many of these problems are directly related to their sexual orientation. If we can't identify these youth, we probably won't be able to help them. The first step is being able to talk about sexuality concerns with any youth under your care.

Sexuality Counseling

Don't be afraid to talk with youth about sexuality issues. You do not incur any liability for doing so. Initial interviews should include questions about the youth's sexuality just as they include other issues that affect their life (i.e., family, school, substance use, suicide, and depression). It is appropriate to do further sexuality counseling with a young person if you have a good relationship with him/her and necessary if you feel that sexuality conflicts are an important part of the situation. It is good to examine your own attitudes and minimize prejudices so that youth can feel free to convey their feelings and experiences to you. The principle of nonjudgmental therapeutic intervention is especially important in working with gay and lesbian youth. Feel comfortable with your own sexuality in order to keep tensions between you and your client to a minimum.

Sexual Orientation

Don't be afraid to ask youth directly about their sexual orientation. Sexual orientation should be routinely included in questions and discussions related to sexuality concerns. Some youth will volunteer the information that they have a gay or lesbian orientation. If you strongly feel that a youth is gay, the only way to find out may be simply to ask. This does not reflect negatively on you, and your intuition is often correct. Even if you are wrong, it rarely hurts your rapport with the youth if approached in a sensitive way. If you are unable to broach the subject with them, it is most likely a reflection of your own discomfort with the issue. Remember that one of the greatest risk factors in the problem gay youth face is the wall of silence surrounding the subject. The silence needs to be broken if you are to enter the lonely place where many gay and lesbian youth reside. It may be good to let youth know in some way that you accept young people regardless of their sexual orientation before asking them. Be prepared to give youth accurate and positive information about homosexuality. Assure them it is a healthy and positive form of human expression. Gay youth will be listening closely.

Acceptance

Accept the youth's sexual orientation as they report it to you. Their sexual identity should be based on the self-reporting of their feelings and experiences. Do not label a youth as heterosexual or homosexual based on your own assumptions. Assure gay youth it is not sick, bad, or wrong for them to be the way they are and that you are not going to try and change them. Let them know you care about them just as much after the disclosure as before. They are used to being rejected by others who find out they are gay. Respect them for being open and honest with you. It was probably hard for them to do and shows that they trust you.

Sexual Orientation Confusion

Do not assume a youth is confused about their sexual orientation if they identify as gay or bisexual. Many people both gay and straight have trouble accepting that an individual is bisexual. It is important to validate bisexuality as a viable option for youth. However, some youth are genuinely confused about their sexual orientation. It is important for them to know that it is all right to be confused. They should not feel pressured to label themselves one way or another. A useful method in helping them to clarify a confused or undecided orientation is the Kinsey Percentage Scale. This technique allows the youth to be any combination of homosexual and heterosexual feelings and experiences that adds up to 100 percent. They can be 85 percent straight and 15 percent gay. Or they can be 40 percent straight and 60 percent gay. It is important to let them know you will accept them no matter where they fall on this scale. The purpose of this method is to give youth a context that allows them to identify their orientation along a continuum. It is easy to move from here to discussing specific feelings and experiences with them.

Gender Identity

Assure effeminate young gay males and masculine young lesbians that it is all right for them to be that way. Gender nonconformity is common among gay youth and may be a way for them to affirm their identity. Some gay youth, however, become confused by cultural stereotypes that insist gay men be like women and lesbians be like men. They feel they actually have to be a person of the opposite gender in order to be gay. Be prepared to talk with them about their perceptions of what it is like being a young gay male or lesbian. Help them to separate social adaptation issues from whether they really believe they are a person of the opposite sex. Assure them they do not have to be any particular way in order to be gay. Transsexual youth will express a persistent desire to be a person of the opposite sex and live as that person over time. They will engage in frequent cross-dressing and adopt the name of a person of the opposite sex. It is important for you to accept these youth for who they believe they are and call them by the name they want to be called. This is critical to establishing basic rapport with these youth and effectively addressing their concerns.

Self-Esteem

Gay and lesbian youth frequently suffer from low self-esteem. They have often received a disproportionate amount of negative attention because of their sexuality. Being gay has been the focus of problems and stigmatization for them. Assure them there is nothing wrong with being gay and that it is the response of others to homosexuals that is the source of the problem. Help them to develop pride in who they are and a positive identity as a gay male or lesbian. Sometimes they have had too much of their identity focused on their sexuality. It is easy for them to come to see themselves as sexual beings after becoming known as homosexuals. Assure them that sexuality is only part of who they are. Explore other areas of potential growth that give them a broader understanding of themselves as individuals. Know the potential of gay youth under your care and work with them in a way that allows them to achieve more success than failure. Give positive feedback whenever possible. Be confident and optimistic of their ability to improve their situation and lead stable and happy lives as gay male and lesbian adults.

Family

Gay and lesbian youth sometimes mistake their parents' inability to accept their sexual orientation as a rejection of them as individuals. Frequently, parents still love their child but need time to come to understand and accept them as gay. Gay youth have trouble recognizing that an initial negative reaction by parents may change in the future. Help families to clarify their feelings for each other and encourage gay youth to be patient in gaining acceptance. Those gay and lesbian youth who have not come out to their parents should not be pressured to do so. It is a personal decision that they should make carefully. Finally, assure gay and lesbian youth that they too will have families as adults. While not the traditional family, their families will be comprised of those friends, lovers, and relatives who remain close with them over a long period of time. Their relationships can be as rich and rewarding as those of other people. Being a gay male or lesbian does not mean that you are going to be alone.

REFERENCES

1. Jay, K., and Young, A. (Eds.) (1977). *The gay report: Lesbians and gay men speak out about their sexual experiences and lifestyles.* New York: Summit.

2. Bell, A., and Weinberg, M. (1978). *Homosexualities: A study of diversity among men and women.* New York: Simon & Schuster.

3. Centers for Disease Control, Center for Environmental Health (1986). *Youth suicide surveillance report.* Atlanta: Department of Health and Human Services.

4. Avicolli, T. (1986, May 9). Coming out of the Dark Ages: Social workers told of special youth needs. *Philadelphia Gay News.*

5. Remafedi, G. (1985). *Male homosexuality: The adolescent's perspective.* Unpublished manuscript, Adolescent Health Program, University of Minnesota.

6. Roesler, T., and Deisher, R. (1972, February 21). Youthful man homosexuality. *Journal of the American Medical Association,* 1018–1023.

7. Los Angeles Suicide Prevention Center (1986). [Problems of suicide among lesbian and gay adolescents.] Unpublished preliminary data.

8. Larkin Street Youth Center (1984). Client statistics. San Francisco.

9. Huckleberry House (1982). Client statistics. San Francisco.

10. National Gay Task Force (1984). *Anti–gay/lesbian victimization.* New York: Author.

11. San Francisco Juvenile Justice Commission (1982). *Problems for gay and lesbian youth involved with the juvenile court.* San Francisco.

12. Wilson, H., community activist and cofounder of the Gay and Lesbian Teachers Coalition. Personal interview, San Francisco, 1986.

13. Rofes, E. (1983). *"I thought people like that killed themselves": Lesbians, gay men and suicide.* San Francisco: Grey Fox.

14. The Bronski Beat (1984). The song "Smalltown Boy" from the album *Age of Consent.* MCA Records.

15. Bell A., Weinberg, M., and Hammersmith, S. (1981). *Sexual preference: Its development in men and women.* Bloomington, IN: Indiana University Press.

16. National Gay Task Force (1978). *Twenty questions about homosexuality.* New York: Author.

17. Kinsey, A., Pomeroy, W., and Martin, C. (1948). *Sexual behavior in the human male.* Philadelphia: Saunders.

18. Kinsey, A., Pomeroy, W., Martin, C., and Gebhard, P. (1953). *Sexual behavior in the human female.* Philadelphia: Saunders.

19. Parris, F. (1985, May 17). Some die young. *Washington Blade.*

20. Morin, S., and Miller, J. (1977). *On fostering positive identity in gay men: Some developmental issues.* Unpublished manuscript, San Francisco.

21. Gibson, P. (1983). Developing services to gay and lesbian youth. In S. Bergstrom, and L. Cruz (Eds.), *Counseling lesbian and gay male youth: Their special needs/special Lives.* National Network of Runaway and Youth Services.

22. Lewis, L. (1984, September–October). The coming-out process for lesbians: Integrating a stable identity. *Social Work,* 464–469.

23. Fourteen-year-old gay male. Personal interview, Berkeley, CA, 1986.

24. Martin, A. (1982). Learning to hide: The socialization of the gay adolescent. *Adolescent Psychiatry, 10,* 52–65.

25. American Psychiatric Association (1980). *The diagnostic and statistical manual of mental disorders* (3rd ed.). Washington, DC: Author.

26. Fricke, A. (1981). *Reflections of a rock lobster: A story about growing up gay.* Boston: Alyson.

27. Weinberg, M., and Williams, C. (1974). *Male homosexuals: Their problems and adaptions.* New York: Oxford.

28. Heron, A. (Ed.) (1983). *One teenager in ten: Writings by gay and lesbian youth.* Boston: Alyson.

29. Hughes, R., program coordinator for Gay and Lesbian Youth Services, Center for Special Problems. Personal interviews, San Francisco, 1986.

30. Davis, R. (1979). Black suicide in the seventies: Current trends. *Suicide and Life-Threatening Behavior, 9,* 3.

31. Hendin, H. (1969). Black suicide. *Archives of General Psychiatry, 2,* 4,

32. Dutton, T. (c. 1977). Nigger in the woodpile. *Fag Rag.*

33. Jones, A. (1983). The need for cultural sensitivity in working with Third World lesbian and gay youth. In S. Bergstrom and L. Cruz (Eds.), *Counseling lesbian and gay male youth: Their special needs/special lives.* National Network of Runaway and Youth Services.

34. Huxdly, J., and Brandon, S. (1981). Partnership in transsexualism: Part I. Paired and non-paired groups. *Archives of Sexual Behavior, 10,* 133–141.

35. Harry, J. (1986, May 8–9). *Adolescent suicide and sexual identity issues.* Paper submitted for the Secretary's Conference on Adolescent Suicide, National Institute of Mental Health , Washington, DC.

36. Heller, J. (1983). *Suicide and sexual issues.* (Place unknown): Suicide Prevention Center, Inc.

37. Gock, T. (1984). *Suicidal homosexual theory as a case of anti–gay/lesbian violence.* Paper presented at the 112th American Public Health Association Meeting , Anaheim, CA.

38. National Gay Task Force (1982). *Gay rights in the United States and Canada.* New York: Author.

39. Wandrei, K. (1985). *Sexual orientation and female suicide attempters.* Unpublished manuscript, Oakland, CA.

40. Suicide at sixteen (1977, January 20–February 3). *Newswest.*

41. Tartagni, D. (1978). Counseling gays in a school setting. *School Counselor, 26,* 26–32.

42. Morrison, M. (1985). *Adolescence and vulnerability to chemical dependence.* Unpublished manuscript.

43. Urban and Rural Systems Associates, U.S. Department of Health and Human Services (1982). *Adolescent male prostitution.* San Francisco: Author.

44. Kassler, J. (1983). *Gay men's health.* New York: Harper & Row.

45. Planned Parenthood (1985). *Teenage sexuality fact sheet.* San Francisco: Author.

Parasuicide, Gender, and Gender Deviance

JOSEPH HARRY
Northern Illinois University

From the *Journal of Health and Social Behavior, 24*
(December 1983), 350–361

ABSTRACT: *The hypotheses that gender-role nonconformity during childhood is associated with social isolation, which in turn is related to subsequent suicidal feelings and attempts, were tested. These ideas were explored in a four-group sample of homosexual and heterosexual men and women living in San Francisco. The data indicated that there was support for the hypotheses; however, childhood gender-role nonconformity was more consequential for the later suicidality of men than of women. The data indicated consistently that gender deviance was more benign in women than in men.*

Few values are as intensely and ubiquitously held as those of gender. The norms governing gender-appropriate behavior widely serve as personal standards for judging the gender adequacy of both self and others. While there is some variation in the contents of gender roles by sex and social class (Duncan & Duncan, 1978), there are probably few individuals who are indifferent to the norms of gender, regardless of their concrete understanding of those norms. The valuing of gender has often given rise to derivative negative concepts of the characteristics of gender deviants, together with the application of childhood terms such as "tomboy" and "sissy" and their adult eroticized versions of "dyke" and "faggot." Such labels depict negative reference persons whom one is not supposed to resemble (Merton, 1957:354–55). Gender deviance is defined here as behavior that violates the norms for gender-appropriate behavior; this deviance is to be distinguished from sexual deviance, which may or may not also be gender deviant. Thus, while transvestites and homosexuals are gender deviant, prostitutes and rapists are sexual deviants who are quite gender conventional.

Gender is valued so intensely that many persons are willing to kill or die in defense of their gender adequacy. The data on male homicides show that a large number of such deaths arose out of often trivial imputations of gender inadequacy by one male to another (Luckenbill, 1977; Wolfgang & Ferracutti, 1982:305–306). While women seem considerably less likely to kill as a result of imputed gender incompetence, their relatively greater propensity to kill spouses, lovers, and sex rivals may also be interpreted as efforts to avenge threats to their adequacy as women in personal relationships. The thrust of the present work is to show that gender deviance may also be a contributing factor in an individual's suicidal propensities.

One's adequacy in a gender role is a major component of one's self-evaluation. Concerns about one's gender adequacy seem to be more common during preadulthood, when persons are learning and attempting to conform to a gender role, rather than during adulthood, by which time most persons have reached an accommodation with a gender role. Boys seem particularly sensitive to questions of gender inadequacy. Tuddenham (1952) found that boys in grades one to five describe themselves as "real boys" more often than they mention any other trait, with degree of athletic skill being the major criterion for whether or not one is a "real boy." Similarly, Stein and Hoffman (1978) found that athletic inability was often a source of self-doubt among adolescent males and led them to question their own masculinity.

Gender-role nonconformity, and particularly that form of nonconformity expressed in engaging in cross-gender activities, has often been found to be associated with rejection by peers during preadulthood. Kagan and Moss (1962:158) reported that "those children who preferred to play with opposite-sex peers during this time [ages 6 to 10] were often rejected by peers of the same sex." Such rejection by peers of children who engage in cross-gender behavior has also been found among preschool children and in the recalled childhood of male homosexuals who engaged in considerable cross-gender activities during that period (Fagot, 1977; Saghir & Robins, 1973:19–20). A consequence of such rejection seems to be that gender-role nonconforming children are often loners and are systematically excluded from the group activities of other preadults, e.g., athletic teams and parties.

The principal hypothesis of the present work is that the isolation associated with rejection due to gender inadequacy during preadulthood may become a persistent pattern and enhance the likelihood of subsequent suicidal behaviors and feelings. One of the more reliable correlates of suicide in the literature seems to be social isolation (Jacobs, 1971; Maris, 1981:112–14; Trout, 1980). The socially isolated individual lacks the usual peer supports that help one deal with the normal strains of life. Hence, lesser problems may become major ones and temporary difficulties may become enduring ones. With a history of self-doubt concerning their gender-adequacy, such isolated individuals seem prepared to respond to life problems with nonconventional reactions. It is important to note that such isolation of the gender-unconventional individual need not arise out of explicit rejection by peers. While children are often quite unrestrained in teasing nonconforming peers, the gender-unconventional individual may come to doubt her/his adequacy through the normal self-other comparisons that are daily engaged in. Also, a measure of self-isolation may arise if the nonconventional preadult is simply uninterested in the sex-typed activity options typically made available to preadults, e.g., sports, arts, and various games.

It has often been argued that gender conformity is positively associated with social adjustment and self-esteem. However, Pleck's (1982) recent review of this literature showed that the findings are mixed. Adjustment may be better related to conformity during preadulthood than during adulthood. Mussen (1961) found that adolescent males who were more masculine, as measured by the Strong Vocational Interest Blank Test, were better socially adjusted during adolescence but were less well-adjusted during early adulthood. It appeared that their success in masculinity during adolescence seemed somewhat incompatible with being an adult male. The studies by Gray (1957) and Webb (1963) reported positive associations of sex-typing in grade school boys, as measured by peer ratings and the Gough Fe scale and by measures of social adjustment/acceptance, respectively.

However, for girls, the association of sex-typing and social adjustment were negative for some of the measures of acceptance, suggesting that sex-typing may be more important for the adjustment of boys than that of girls.

While the measures of psychological masculinity and femininity of Bem (1974) and of Spence and Helmreich (1978) have been found to be reliably associated with adult and adolescent self-esteem (Kelly & Worrell, 1977), there is considerable question about whether these scales in fact measure the sets of cultural activities embodied in gender roles. These scales were found to have essentially no associations with the California Personality Inventory Femininity Scale, which consists of activities typically prescribed for one sex or the other (Spence & Helmreich, 1978:21–22). Rather than conceptualizing these scales as masculinity and femininity, it might be better to see them as measuring aggressiveness and expressiveness, while reserving the former concepts for cultural (role) rather than psychological phenomena.

While the working hypothesis of the present work is that early gender-role nonconformity may lead to social isolation — with or without rejection — and a subsequently enhanced possibility of suicide, it is probably necessary to qualify this hypothesis by gender. Gender-role nonconformity seems less disapproved among women than among men. Duncan and Duncan (1978:272) found in a national survey that "It was more important to these fathers that a boy act like a boy should than a girl act like a girl should." Consistent with this, others (Goldstein & Oldham, 1979:127–28; Kohlberg & Zigler, 1967) have found that grade school boys are considerably greater gender-role conformists in their expressed activity and occupational preferences than are grade school girls. While some girls are occasionally negatively sanctioned for tomboyish behaviors, such behaviors do not seem to evoke the intense disapproval and concern evoked by cross-gender behaviors in boys (Saghir & Robins, 1973:18–20, 192–194). Hence, one might expect to find less association between cross-gender behaviors and isolation in females than in males.

The empirical literature on suicidal phenomena seems bifurcated into that dealing with completed suicides and that dealing with attempted suicides and suicidal ideation. While the latter phenomena have at times been treated as predicative of or precursors of the former, estimates indicate that only five to ten percent of attempters eventually become completers (deCataranzo, 1981:171–72; Farberow, 1977). Also, the demographic characteristics of completers and attempters differ considerably, with the former typically being middle-aged and male and the latter often being in their 20s and female (Kreiman, 1977:119, 161; Maris, 1981:39–45). Given these differences, some authors have suggested that attempters and completers are substantially, although not completely, different populations and have labeled those who only attempt suicide or express suicidal feelings as "parasuicides" (deCataranzo, 1981:165–74; Kreitman, 1977:1–4).

Given the likely different populations of suicides and parasuicides, the hypothesis that gender-role nonconformity and isolation are associated with subsequent suicidality may bear more on parasuicide than on suicide. The nonconformity and isolation discussed here are phenomena of preadulthood and temporally much closer to the risk period of attempted suicides. While nonconformity and isolation may also eventuate in ultimate suicide, proximate effects often seem more credible than do much more distant ones. Hence, the analyses that follow are limited to the associations of parasuicide with preadult gender-role nonconformity and social isolation.

In summary, the hypotheses at hand are:

1. Childhood gender-role conformity is associated with social isolation.
2. Such isolation is associated with suicidal feelings and attempts.
3. Gender-role nonconformity may be more consequential for isolation and parasuicide among males than among females.

RESEARCH METHODS

Sample

Because childhood cross-gendering is so strongly related to sexual orientation among both males and females, it would be difficult to acquire a sufficient number of persons with a history of cross-gendering in a representative probability sample of the general population. The sample employed here attempts to overcome this difficulty by oversampling the segment of the population with the greatest incidence of childhood cross-gendering, i.e., homosexuals. The data for the present work were provided by the Kinsey Institute of Indiana University and consist of their San Francisco survey of 686 homosex-

TABLE 1. Percentage Distribution of Sample Groups by Demographic Variables

Demographic Variables	Sample Group			
	Gay Males (n=686)	Heterosexual Males (n=337)	Lesbians (n=293)	Heterosexual Females (n=140)
Education				
−12 yrs.	25	26	24	26
13–15 yrs.	36	34	36	37
16 yrs. +	39	40	40	37
White	84	84	78	72
Age				
−24 yrs.	22	23	19	28
25–34 yrs.	32	33	36	34
35–44 yrs.	23	20	23	19
45–54 yrs.	16	14	20	12
55 yrs. +	7	10	2	7

ual males, 337 heterosexual males, 293 homosexual females, and 140 heterosexual females. The data are based on two- to five-hour interviews conducted in the fall of 1969 and the spring of 1970. A detailed description of the sampling methods has been presented by others (Bell & Weinberg, 1978:30–44). A discussion of the possibility of changes in gender roles since the gathering of these data is deferred until later.

A large pool of several thousand homosexual volunteers for interviewing was acquired from a wide variety of sources in the San Francisco area. These volunteers were stratified by age, sex, race, and education. Sampling was then done within each of these strata so as to create heterogeneity on these demographic variables, and the selected homosexual respondents were interviewed in the fall of 1969. Then a comparable sample of heterosexual respondents was selected from the Bay Area through probability sampling of census tracts and blocks and quota sampling within blocks. The quotas employed within blocks were designed to equate the gay and heterosexual respondents on age, race, and education within each sex. Because the heterosexual respondents were standardized on the homosexual demographics within each sex, the heterosexuals should not be taken as a probability sample of San Francisco area residents. The demographics for the four sample groups are presented in Table 1. The interviewing of the heterosexual respondents was completed in the spring of 1970.

Measures

Suicidality-parasuicide was measured by the following series of questions: "Have you ever imagined yourself committing suicide (not necessarily seriously)?"; if yes, "Have you ever seriously considered committing suicide?"; if yes, "How many times have you tried it?"; and "How old were you when you tried it the first time?" Since the number of heterosexual respondents who had actually attempted suicide was somewhat small, the attempters and serious considerers were combined into a single category for the statistical analyses. The measure of suicidality consisted of the three categories of: (1) attempted or seriously considered, (2) only imagined, and (3) neither attempted, considered, nor imagined. However, since the interested reader may wish to distinguish actual attempters from serious considerers, the percentages for the former are also presented. The measure of social isolation employed for adolescence was "During these years (high school), to what extent were you a loner?"; the response categories were "Very Much," "Some," "Very Little," and "Not at All."

The measure of childhood gender-role nonconformity consisted of the following items: During grade school, "To what extent did you enjoy specifically the boys' activities (e.g., baseball, football)?"; "To what extent did you enjoy specifically girls' activities (e.g., hopscotch, playing house, jacks)?" The response categories for these two items were "Very Much," "Somewhat," "Very Little," and "Not at All." The scale also included the third item of a self-rating as "Masculine" versus "Feminine" as descriptive of "the kind of person you were during the time you were growing up (until age 17)." The alpha reliabilities for this scale are 0.69 among males and 0.71 among females. The scale probably measures the slightly narrower concept of cross-gendering than the broader one of gender-role nonconformity, since it is possible for an individual to be a nonconformist, e.g., a boy disinterested in sports, while not being interested in specifically cross-gender activities. In the tables that follow, the childhood cross-gendering scale has been dichotomized at the respective median for each sex.

Since the measure of childhood cross-gendering involves long-distance recall data, some discussion of its validity is in order. Scales of childhood cross-gendering similar to the present one have been repeat-

edly and reliably employed to distinguish homosexuals from heterosexuals at several places in the United States and in other countries
(Bell et al., 1981:75–77, 147–48; Freund, 1974; Harry, 1982:63;
Saghir & Robins, 1973:19, 193; Whitam, 1977, 1980). Typically, the
differences found have been quite large — on the order of 60 to 70
percentage points. Hence, only the validity of such scales may be
seriously questionable. Bearing on the validity of such recalled cross-
gendering is the great similarity of the cross-gendered childhood
recalled by adults to the direct observations by researchers of effeminate boys and cross-gendered girls (Green, 1976; Green et al., 1982;
Zuger, 1966). The similarities of recalled and observed cross-gendering include, among males, the trait of a major and persistent interest
in acting or dramatic portrayals (Green & Money, 1966; Harry,
1982:52–53; Whitam, 1977). While the meaning of this major correlate of childhood cross-gendering is presently incompletely understood, the significance of this odd trait for the question of validity
seems to be that it is rather unlikely that such a peculiar trait would
arise in adult recalls of childhood cross-gendering without a basis in
reality. Other characteristics typical of recalled childhood cross-gendering are the vividness and bitterness with which they are recalled
(Saghir & Robins, 1973:19–20), characteristics that suggest that such
recalls do not have a social reconstructionist mythic quality.

   A more problematic potential invalidity problem is that homosexuals may be more willing to recall childhood cross-gendering than are
heterosexuals. Such differential validity may arise because there are
probably stronger norms among heterosexuals than among homosexuals to appear gender conformist, both in their present and past. While
such differential intensity of norms probably exists, it should be noted
that there are also considerable normative supports for appearing
gender conformist among homosexuals. Humphreys (1971) has reported that within the last 15 years, there have developed norms of
masculine self-deportment among gay men. Similarly, this researcher
has encountered that when lines of questioning or discussion about
childhood cross-gendering are included in questionnaires or discussions directed to homosexual audiences, some irritated or hostile
responses, or nonresponses, are inevitable. Such limited evidence
bearing on the differential validity of cross-gendering scales among
heterosexual and homosexual populations cannot definitely resolve

the validity question; the latter must remain until longitudinal studies of cross-gendered children currently in process (Green, 1980) are completed.

In the present data, it was possible to deal directly with the hypothesis that persons who report cross-gendering during childhood might have been influenced by the writings of psychiatrists and social scientists on the presence of cross-gendering in the childhood of homosexuals. Among homosexual respondents, no relationships appear between the cross-gendering scale and exposure to "books, articles or lectures on homosexuality ever read or heard by medical doctors or social scientists." This question was not asked of heterosexual respondents.

Analyses

Log-linear analyses were employed. In the tables that follow, variables are referred to by letters, and associations between variables are referred to by pairs of letters. Interaction terms are represented by combinations of three or more letters. Partial associations are referred to by expressions such as CL.S and AC.SL. In short, the notation for partial correlation has been adopted. The leftmost chi-squareds presented refer to the partial associations, while the rightmost refer to the zero-order ones. The statistical analyses employed the BMDP log-linear analysis program (Brown, 1977).

RESULTS

Table 2 presents adolescent loner by childhood cross-gendering by sexual orientation for males and females. The strongest associations in this table are those between sexual orientation and childhood cross-gendering. However, these associations are considered to be exogenous here, and they cannot readily be explained within the present data, although Bell et al. (1981) attempted this. Of interest here are the positive associations between childhood cross-gendering and being an adolescent loner. Among the males, both childhood cross-gendering and sexual orientation, when one or the other is controlled, are associated with adolescent loner. That sexual orientation remains associated with adolescent loner after childhood cross-gendering is controlled suggests that sexual orientation also may

TABLE 2. Adolescent Loner by Childhood Cross-Gendering by Sexual Orientation for Males and Females (Percentage)

Males			
Sexual Orientation (S)	Childhood Cross-Gendering (C)	Percentage Loners (L)	N (100%)*
Gay	Low	60	195
	High	71	488
Heterosexual	Low	48	308
	High	72	29

Partial Associations				Marginal Associations	
Effect	df	LR Chi-Squared	p	LR Chi-Squared	p
LC.S	1	11.62	.001	35.56	.001
LS.C	1	5.98	.014	29.92	.001
CS.L	1	372.53	.001	396.47	.001
LCS	1	1.47	.225		

Females			
Sexual Orientation (S)	Childhood Cross-Gendering (C)	Percentage Loners (L)	N (100%)
Gay	Low	59	61
	High	62	232
Heterosexual	Low	41	100
	High	55	40

Partial Associations				Marginal Associations	
Effect	df	LR Chi-Squared	p	LR Chi-Squared	p
LC.S	1	1.76	.185	7.51	.006
LS.C	1	4.98	.026	10.73	.001
CS.L	1	97.50	.001	103.25	.001
LCS	1	0.74			

*Three homosexual males provided incomplete response on the Childhood Cross-Gendering items.

contribute to alienation from peers, since it is during adolescence that gays and lesbians first become intensely aware of their attractions to the same sex — and this is often a matter of considerable confusion and guilt (Saghir & Robins, 1973:38–41, 208–11). The findings for the females differ somewhat from those for the males in that, although childhood cross-gendering is positively associated with adolescent loner at the zero-order level, this association vanishes once sexual orientation is controlled. Among the males, the zero-order and partial gammas of cross-gendering with adolescent loner are 0.37 and 0.25, respectively, while among the females, they are 0.27 and 0.12. These data suggest that cross-gendering among females is less alienating from peers than among males. As discussed earlier, there may be greater tolerance of gender nonconformity for women than for men.

Other indicators of alienation were also found to display patterns of association similar to that of adolescent loner. Responses to the question during high school "to what extent did you feel left out?" were found to be strongly associated with adolescent loner for all four groups defined in terms of sex and sexual orientation, with gammas on the order of 0.70. Feeling left out was also found to be associated with childhood cross-gendering among both male groups but not among the female groups, again indicating the lesser alienating influence of cross-gendering among females than among males.

That childhood cross-gendering is associated with considerable adolescent unhappiness is shown in Table 3, which presents responses to the question "During this period of your life (high school) were you very happy, pretty happy, not too happy, or were you very unhappy?" by childhood cross-gendering and sexual orientation for males and females. Among the males, cross-gendering is associated with later unhappiness, both before and after sexual orientation is controlled, while among the females, the positive zero-order association of cross-gendering with unhappiness vanishes after sexual orientation is controlled. The respective zero-order and partial gammas of cross-gendering with unhappiness among the males are 0.40 and 0.35, while among the females, they are 0.34 and 0.14. Again, these data indicate that cross-gendering has more potential for unhappiness among the males than among the females.

Table 3 also shows a significant interaction for the males. Cross-gendering is more strongly associated with adolescent unhappiness for the heterosexual than for the homosexual males. Differently stated, sexual orientation has no association with unhappiness among the non-cross-gendered while it does have an association among the cross-gendered. The data suggest that cross-gendering may be more incompatible with the self-definitions of the heterosexual males than with those of the homosexual males. Gender-role nonconformity, while it occurs far less often in the childhood of heterosexual males,

TABLE 3. Adolescent Happiness by Childhood Cross-Gendering and Sexual
Orientation for Males and Females (Percentage)

Males			
Sexual Orientation (S)	Childhood Cross-Gendering (C)	Percentage Happy (H)	N (100%)
Gay	Low	70	195
	High	55	488
Heterosexual	Low	75	308
	High	38	29

Partial Associations				Marginal Associations	
Effect	df	LR Chi-Squared	p	LR Chi-Squared	p
HC.S	1	25.10	.001	40.83	.001
HS.C	1	0.06	.805	15.79	.001
HCS	1	4.72	.030		

Females			
Sexual Orientation (S)	Childhood Cross-Gendering (C)	Percentage Happy (H)	N (100%)
Gay	Low	52	61
	High	47	232
Heterosexual	Low	75	100
	High	62	40

Partial Associations				Marginal Associations	
Effect	df	LR Chi-Squared	p	LR Chi-Squared	p
HC.S	1	2.04	.154	11.60	.001
HS.C	1	10.91	.001	20.48	.001
HCS	1	0.63	.428		

seems crucial to their adolescent affective states. As might be expected, adolescent loner and adolescent unhappiness were found to be strongly associated among all four groups defined in terms of sex and sexual orientation.

Table 4 presents parasuicide by adolescent loner by childhood cross-gendering by sexual orientation for males and females.[1] The data show that for the males, parasuicide is significantly associated with adolescent loner, childhood cross-gendering, and sexual orientation, both at the zero-order and second-order partial levels. Adolescent loner is clearly the strongest of these associations, while the other two associations are considerably weakened in the partials. The pattern of

TABLE 4. Parasuicide by Adolescent Loner by Childhood Cross-Gendering by Sexual Orientation for Males and Females (Percentage)

Males

Sexual Orientation (S)	Childhood Cross-Gendering (C)	Adolescent Loner (L)	Parasuicide (A)* Considered/ Attempted	Only Imagined	Neither	N (100%)
Gay	Low	Low	17 (10)	34	49	77
		High	35 (23)	37	28	118
	High	Low	25 (13)	39	35	142
		High	43 (21)	36	20	346
Heterosexual	Low	Low	5 (2)	32	62	160
		High	14 (3)	50	36	148
	High	Low	12 (0)	50	38	8
		High	38 (10)	29	33	21

		Partial Associations			Marginal Associations	
Effect	df	LR Chi-Squared	p		LR Chi-Squared	p
AL.CS	2	50.23	.001		73.38	.001
AC.LS	2	12.02	.002		72.04	.001
AS.LC	2	23.02	.001		81.79	.001
ALC.S	2	1.03	.598			
ALS.C	2	0.16	.924			
ACS.L	2	3.86	.145			
ALCS	2	1.38	.501			

Females

Sexual Orientation (S)	Childhood Cross-Gendering (C)	Adolescent Loner (L)	Parasuicide (A)* Considered/ Attempted	Only Imagined	Neither	N (100%)
Gay	Low	Low	24 (8)	44	32	25
		High	44 (28)	28	28	36
	High	Low	23 (16)	33	44	87
		High	47 (30)	34	19	145
Heterosexual	Low	Low	22 (10)	32	46	59
		High	24 (7)	46	29	41
	High	Low	17 (11)	50	33	18
		High	33 (24)	29	38	21

		Partial Associations			Marginal Associations	
Effect	df	LR Chi-Squared	p		LR Chi-Squared	p
AL.CS	2	19.52	.001		23.09	.001
AC.LS	2	0.06	.971		3.35	.188
AS.LC	2	3.70	.156		8.64	.013
ALC.S	2	0.56	.757			
ALS.C	2	1.10	.577			
ACS.L	2	0.04	.980			
ALCS	2	5.70	.058			

*The percentages who had actually attempted suicide are presented in parentheses, although the significance tests were performed with the suicide measure trichotomized.

associations among the females is considerably different. While both adolescent loner and sexual orientation have significant zero-order associations with parasuicide, only adolescent loner has a direct partial link with parasuicide, and childhood cross-gendering has neither zero-order nor partial associations with parasuicide. The respective zero-order and second-order partial gammas of cross-gendering with parasuicide among the males are 0.41 and 0.20, while among the females, they are 0.15 and 0.04. The corresponding gamma coefficients for adolescent loner with parasuicide are 0.44, 0.38, 0.37, and 0.41. Thus, it seems that cross-gendering may have more benign outcomes among women than among men and that, at least among the women, adolescent loner is a more significant correlate of parasuicide than is cross-gendering.

The associations between sexual orientation and suicidality shown in Table 4 suggest the possibility that some of the homosexuals may have been prompted toward suicide or suicidal feelings by the negative views toward homosexuality held by the society at large (Levitt & Klassen, 1974). Many young lesbians and gays react to their early homosexual feelings, which typically occur during adolescence, with a variety of negative feelings (Dank, 1971; Harry & DeVall, 1978:68), since they are still very largely isolated from other homosexuals and must rely on the societal views of homosexuality for their impressions. This possibility was explored by analyzing responses to the following set of questions, which were asked only of the lesbian and gay respondents: "How old were you when you first began to think of yourself as being sexually different?"; "How old were you when you labeled the difference you felt 'homosexual'?"; "How did you feel about this?" Responses to the last of these questions were grouped into those that were positive or neutral and those that were negative. Table 5 presents suicidality by feelings about one's incipient homosexuality by childhood cross-gendering for the gay and lesbian respondents. These data reveal that for both males and females, negative feelings about one's incipient homosexuality are associated with suicidal feelings and may explain some of the suicidal attempts that occur during late adolescence and early adulthood. Among the males, the respective zero-order and partial gammas for the association of negative feelings and parasuicide are 0.18 and 0.17, while among the females, they are 0.27 and 0.25.

TABLE 5. Parasuicide by Negative Feelings about Homosexuality by Childhood Cross-Gendering for Gay Males and Lesbians (Percentage)

Gay Males					
		Parasuicide (A)*			
Childhood Cross-Gendering (C)	Feelings (F)	Considered/Attempted	Only Imagined	Neither	N (100%)†
Low	Accepting	23 (17)	28	49	78
	Negative	30 (18)	41	29	111
High	Accepting	33 (18)	41	26	189
	Negative	42 (20)	36	22	291

		Partial Associations		Marginal Associations	
Effect	df	LR Chi-Squared	p	LR Chi-Squared	p
AF.C	2	7.90	.019	8.12	.017
AC.F	2	13.28	.001	13.49	.001
CF.A	1	0.00	.947	0.22	.639
CFA	2	3.94	.139		

Lesbians					
		Parasuicide (A)*			
Childhood Cross-Gendering (C)	Feelings (F)	Considered/Attempted	Only Imagined	Neither	N (100%)†
Low	Accepting	26 (17)	30	44	23
	Negative	44 (24)	35	21	34
High	Accepting	32 (19)	31	36	102
	Negative	42 (29)	36	22	125

		Partial Associations		Marginal Associations	
Effect	df	LR Chi-Squared	p	LR Chi-Squared	p
AF.C	2	9.25	.001	9.18	.010
AC.F	2	0.14	.931	0.07	.965
CF.A	1	0.41	.523	0.34	.562
CFA	2	0.33	.847		

*The percentages who had actually attempted suicide are presented in parentheses, although the significance tests were executed with the parasuicide measure trichotomized.
†Nine lesbians and 14 gay men either felt sexually different or did not label themselves homosexual or did not respond.

DISCUSSION

Since the data analyzed here were gathered in 1969 and 1970, the possibility should be considered that subsequent social changes have altered the phenomena under consideration. First, the gay/lesbian movement of the 1970s has certainly effected significant changes in gay lifestyles and may have had some positive effects on the psychological well-being of adult gays and lesbians and hence on their suicidality (Harry & DeVall, 1978:143–149). Thus, one might anticipate that the homosexual/heterosexual differences in suicidality reported above would be less today. While this is probably true, it should be noted that the variables used as predictors of suicidality in the present analysis, i.e., childhood cross-gendering, adolescent loner, and adolescent unhappiness, come from the preadult period of the respondents' life. Also, a large amount of the suicidality among the homosexual respondents occurs during this period of their life. During this period, homosexual preadults are very largely isolated from the adult gay movement. In the present data, both the gay and lesbian respondents "became a part of a homosexual clique or crowd," i.e., "came out," at a median age of 21 (although 15 percent of the lesbians and 13 percent of the gay men never did). Prior to such coming out, gay and lesbian preadults are almost totally immersed in the larger heterosexual culture and subject to the conventional definitions of and sanctions for gender roles, gender deviance, and sexual orientation. Hence, it may be that changes in heterosexually defined gender roles during the last decade may be more relevant to the present data than are changes associated with the lesbian and gay movement.

While there is considerable evidence that there have been changes in attitudes on gender roles in the last two decades, most of that evidence is on changes in the female role (Thornton & Freedman, 1979). In reviewing changes in attitudes toward gender roles expressed in numerous surveys between the mid-1950s and the mid-1970s, Duncan and Duncan (1978:91) reported that there has been increasing approval of working women and that the changes in favor of including a work component in the female gender role have occurred principally among the young, the educated, and women. While men have also changed their views on the work roles of women, they have changed less and still adopt more gender-conservative views on a variety of gender-related topics. As indicators of gender-role socialization attitudes, these authors also analyzed trend data on the differential allocation of gender-typed tasks to children by sex of the child. The tasks were cleaning the walks, washing the car, dusting the furniture, and making beds. Increasing percentages of respondents between 1953 and 1971 were willing to assign these tasks to children of both sexes, except for the task of dusting, which remained very largely a girl's task. There was also some resistance to change evidenced in attitudes toward making beds. The authors inferred that men seemed increasingly willing to relinquish responsibility for formerly male-typed activities, but they seemed unwilling to incorporate into their own roles formerly female-typed activities.

Tittle's (1981) recent study of high school juniors in New York City presented a factor analysis of a large number of household tasks to be performed by their future spouses, and male and female factors appeared quite clearly. While the male students had come to accept the idea that their future wives would work, they also reported that they would feel negative if their wives earned more than they did. These data suggest that these students had achieved the "liberated" position that wives can work and earn money outside of the household, but not too much of it. It is worth noting that Tittle's study was not done in a small rural town but in New York City where one might have expected gender-role changes to have occurred maximally. The extant literature seems to indicate that most of the changes in sex roles in recent decades have been limited to the female sex role. The male role seems to remain almost totally intact.

If the major changes in definitions of gender roles have principally been ones that broadened the female role in such a way as to incorporate into it formerly male-typed activities, e.g., work and sports, this means that gender deviance among women and girls is either less consequential than earlier or more narrowly defined. However, the lesser consequentiality of gender deviance among women has been one of the principal findings of the present work. Childhood cross-gendering was found to have weaker associations with suicidality, adolescent unhappiness, and adolescent loner among women than among men. Since the data clearly suggest the lesser consequentiality of childhood cross-gendering among women for earlier decades, it seems that more recent data might only show more strongly the differential importance of gender deviance among men and women.

CONCLUSIONS

The data of the present work have shown that departure from gender-appropriate behavior during preadulthood is significant for the individual's subsequent potential for suicidal feelings and attempts. Although such departures are much more common among gays and lesbians, they were found to be associated with suicidality among both heterosexuals and homosexuals. It was also found that early gender deviance was more predictive of subsequent suicidality among men than among women. Gender deviance among males seems to be considerably more punished and alienating from peers than among women. However, it should be noted that gender deviance during adulthood may not be as alienating as during preadulthood, since adults have greater autonomy for selecting their peers and also may have less severely stereotypical views of gender roles than do children and adolescents.

NOTES

Acknowledgment is extended to the Kinsey Institute for the Study of Sex, Gender, and Reproduction for the data here analyzed and for partial support of the present work.

1. The present data on suicide attempts strongly resemble the data of others on the ages at which suicide is attempted. Among the four sample groups, the median ages at which the first actual suicide attempt was made are: homosexual males, 20.2 (N = 127); heterosexual males, 21.2 (N = 10); homosexual females, 21.1 (N = 69); heterosexual females, 19.0 (N = 17). While the percentages of suicide attempts in the present data may seem somewhat high, it should be remembered that the data were gathered in a "suicide capital," San Francisco (Litman et al., 1974).

REFERENCES

Bell, Alan, and Weinberg, Martin (1978). *Homosexualities: A study of diversity among men and women.* New York: Simon & Schuster.

Bell, Alan; Weinberg, Martin; and Hammersmith, Sue (1981). *Sexual preference: Its development in men and women.* Bloomington, IN: Indiana University Press.

Bem, S.L. (1974). The measurement of psychological androgyny. *Journal of Consulting and Clinical Psychology, 42,* 155–62.

Brown, Morton B. (Ed.) (1977). *BMDP biomedical computer programs.* Berkeley, CA: University of California Press.

Dank, B. (1971).Coming out in the gay world. *Psychiatry, 34,* 180–197.

deCataranzo, Denys (1981). *Suicide and self-damaging behavior.* New York: Academic Press.

Duncan, Beverly, and Duncan, Otis (1978). *Sex typing.* New York: Academic Press.

Fagot, B. (1977). Consequences of moderate cross-gender behavior in pre-school children. *Child Development, 48,* 902–907.

Farberow, N. (1977). Suicide. In Edward Sagarin and Fred Montanino (Eds.), *Deviants* (pp. 503–570). Morristown, NJ: General Learning Press.

Freund, K. (1974). Male homosexuality. In John A. Loraine (Ed.), *Understanding homosexuality* (pp. 25–81). New York: Elsevier.

Goldstein, Bernard, and Oldham, Jack (1979). *Children and work.* New Brunswick, NJ: Transaction Books.

Gray, S. (1957). Masculinity-femininity in relation to anxiety and social acceptance. *Child Development, 28,* 203–214.

Green, R. (1980). Patterns of sexual identity in childhood. In Judd Marmor (Ed.), *Homosexual Behavior* (pp. 255–266). New York: Basic Books.

——————— (1976). One hundred ten feminine and masculine boys. *Archives of Sexual Behavior, 5,* 425–446.

Green, R., and Money, J. (1966). Stage-acting, role-taking, and effeminate impersonation during boyhood. *Archives of General Psychiatry, 15,* 535–538.

Green, R., Williams, K., and Goodman, M. (1982). Ninety-nine "tomboys and non-tomboys." *Archives of Sexual Behavior, 11,* 247–266.

Harry, Joseph (1982). *Gay children grown up.* New York: Praeger.

Harry, Joseph, and DeVall, William (1978). *The social organization of gay males.* New York: Praeger.

Humphreys, L. (1971). New styles in homosexual manliness. *Trans-Action, 8,* 38–46.

Jacobs, Jerry (1971). *Adolescent suicide.* New York: Wiley.

Kagan, Jerome, and Moss, Howard (1962). *Birth to maturity.* New York: Wiley.

Kelly, J., and Worrell, J. (1977). New formulations of sex-roles and androgyny. *Journal of Clinical and Consulting Psychology, 45,* 1101–1115.

Kohlberg, L., and Zigler, E. (1967). The impact of cognitive maturity on the development of sex-role attitudes in the years 4 to 8. *Genetic Psychology Monographs, 75,* 89–165.

Kreitman, Norman (Ed.) (1977). *Parasuicide.* New York: Wiley.

Levitt, E., and Klassen, A. (1974). Public attitudes toward homosexuality. *Journal of Homosexuality, 1,* 29–43.

Litman, R., Farberow, N., Wold, C., and Brown, T. (1974). Prediction models of suicidal behavior. In Aaron Beck, Harvey Resnik, and Dan Lettieri (Eds.), *The prediction of suicide* (pp. 141–159). Bowie, MD: The Charles Press Publishers.

Luckenbill, D. (1977). Criminal homicide as a situated transaction. *Social Problems, 25,* 176–186.

Maris, Ronald (1981). *Pathways to suicide.* Baltimore: Johns Hopkins Press.

Merton, Robert (1957). *Social theory and social structure.* New York: Free Press.

Mussen, P. (1961). Some antecedents and consequences of masculine sex-typing in adolescent boys. *Psychological Monographs, 75,* 1–24.

Pleck, Joseph (1982). *The myth of masculinity.* Cambridge, MA: MIT Press.

Saghir, Marcel, and Robins, Eli (1973). *Male and female homosexuality.* Baltimore: Williams & Wilkins.

Spence, Janet, and Helmreich, Robert (1978). *Masculinity and femininity.* Austin, TX: University of Texas Press.

Stein, P., and Hoffman, S. (1978). Sports and male role strain. *Journal of Social Issues, 34,* 48–149.

Thornton, A., and Freedman, D. (1979). Changes in the sex-role attitudes of women. *American Sociological Review, 44,* 832–842.

Tittle, Carol (1981). *Careers and family.* Beverly Hills, CA: Sage.

Trout, D.L. (1980). The role of social isolation in suicide. *Suicide and Life-Threatening Behavior, 10,* 10–23.

Tuddenham, R.D. (1952). Sex and grade differences in school children's evaluation of their peers. *Psychological Monographs, 66*(333), 1–39.

Webb, A.P. (1963). Sex-role preferences and adjustment in early adolescents. *Child Development, 34,* 609–618.

Whitam, F. (1977). Childhood indicators of male homosexuality. *Archives of Sexual Behavior, 6,* 89–96.

——————— (1980). The prehomosexual male child in three societies: The United States, Guatemala, Brazil. *Archives of Sexual Behavior, 9,* 87–99.

Wolfgang, Marvin, and Ferracutti, Franco (1982). *The subculture of violence.* Beverly Hills, CA: Sage.

Zuger, B. (1966). Effeminate behavior in boys from early childhood. *Journal of Pediatrics, 69,* 1098–1107.

Suicide among Homosexual Adolescents

RONALD F.C. KOURANY, M.D.
Vanderbilt University Medical Center

From the *Journal of Homosexuality*, *13*(4) (Summer 1987), 111–117.

ABSTRACT: *Little attention has been given in the professional literature to suicide among homosexual adolescents. Sixty-six adolescent psychiatrists responded to a questionnaire on the subject. Results from this survey suggest that many experts are not working with homosexual adolescents. On the other hand, the majority of those treating them considered them to be at higher risk for suicide and agreed that their suicidal gestures were more severe than those of other adolescents.*

The number of adolescents who are trying to kill themselves is increasing each year. The statistics are troublesome, as suicide is the third leading cause of death among adolescents between the ages of 15 and 19. The suicide rate has risen by about 300% over the past two decades (Holinger, 1978). Explanations of these tragic changes abound. Suicidal adolescents are thought to have a higher incidence of psychiatric disorders like substance abuse, schizophrenia, and affective disorders (Otto, 1972), or to be experiencing socio-environmental stresses such as peer pressures, loss of social values, or poor family support (Williams & Lyons, 1976). General population changes have led to larger proportions of adolescents and, as a consequence, to increases in suicide rates explained partly by increased levels of competition, isolation, and failure among this age group (Holinger &

Offer, 1982). Improved reporting may also account for some of the increases in those rates. Yet little attention has been given in the professional literature to adolescent suicide in the homosexual sub-group. One could hypothesize that due to developmental sociological, familial, and moral tensions, adolescents with a homosexual prefer-ence would be at greater risk for suicide. Yet, the available reported information is very scant.

Although the incidence of suicide among adolescents is increas-ing, systematic study of this phenomenon among homosexual teen-agers, or adolescents who indulge in homosexual behaviors, is prac-tically non-existent. In an effort to evaluate the magnitude of this clinical issue, the author decided to turn to those who treat adoles-cents, get their opinions, and collect their impressions from their patient experiences.

METHOD

Subjects for the study were selected from the 1982 membership directory of the American Society of Adolescent Psychiatry. A subject pool was created by selecting every third member printed in the "Z" section and counting backwards through the "A" section. From this pool a sample of 166 subjects was selected by choosing every tenth subject, beginning with the "A" section and continuing through the "Z" section. This process was continued until the desired number of subjects (N = 166) was attained.

The anonymous questionnaire (a sample of which is available on request) consisted of ten open-ended questions inquiring about sus-pected reasons for suicide attempts in the adolescent population, and then among homosexual adolescents. Other questions focused on the severity and frequency of these attempts. Psychodynamic issues, dis-closures in therapy, and patients' common characteristics were also surveyed.

A total of 66 questionnaires (39.7%) were returned. Most respon-dents were male; only five were female. Their ages ranged from 31 to 65, with a mean of 48.3 years old. Years of experience in practice ranged from 4 to 40, with a mean of 18.33 years. Among the psychia-trists who returned the questionnaires, 18 felt that the subject matter was not applicable to their practices. They made comments like: "I have had no exposure to the homosexual adolescent in my practice"; "I have not seen any homosexual adolescents"; "I do a psychoanalytical practice"; "I have not had any experience with suicidal homosexual adolescents"; "I do not have sufficient experience"; "My experience is too limited"; "None seen, so unable to respond."

RESULTS

Over 65% of the respondents were able to speculate on the reasons for the increase of suicide attempts among adolescents. The most frequently cited cause was family-related: problems in the family — divorce, separation, working parents, poor parental role models. The next most common cause was adolescent intrapsychic distress, which was often described as a sense of isolation, futility, feelings of rejection, rootlessness, and hopelessness, low self-esteem, identity problems, and a lack of direction and goals in life. Social and environmental pressures ranked next, including stress and communication problems at school or with peers. Other less frequently mentioned causes included psychiatric disorders like depression, character disorders, or schizophrenia. Exposure to the idea of suicide in the media, with suicide being portrayed as "more acceptable" and thus more "infectious," was brought up by a few respondents. Drug and alcohol abuse were also listed as causative factors leading to suicide.

When asked to comment about the suicidal gestures among homosexual adolescents, nearly 60% of the respondents (n = 39) said they had no experience or opinion on the subject. Those with experience (n = 27) considered the risk of suicide to be generally higher among these adolescents, particularly those who experienced a sense of disenfranchisement, social isolation, rejection from family or peers, or self-revulsion. And the respondents felt ego-dystonic homosexuals were at higher risk for suicide.

Many psychiatrists, 66% of the respondents to this question, considered suicidal gestures by homosexual adolescents more serious and more lethal than similar ones by the heterosexual group. Only four expressed opinions to the contrary. More than half (55%) did not offer an answer to this question. The respondents felt that the association of homosexuality with suicidal behavior could happen at any particular point in the course of therapy, either early or late. Some felt it never came about, and a few had treated patients who had already made the association prior to the initiation of treatment.

Feelings of rejection was the most common response given by these professionals as to the reason for suicide attempts in the homosexual group. Self-hate, rage, and depression were the next most frequent factors thought to contribute to suicidal behavior. Identity problems, dependency conflicts, "narcissistic vulnerability," feelings of shame, embarrassment, guilt, and humiliation followed in frequency. Other less-often mentioned causes included homophobia, feelings of being different, fear of failure, and a plea for help.

The respondents felt that this group of adolescents, like their heterosexual counterparts, shared the burden of family, peer, and school problems, but also had increased dependency needs and an increased sense of isolation due to not being accepted and to being different. Splitting, immature, primitive, narcissistic defenses were mentioned as primary coping mechanisms. More than half of all the respondents (57%) did not express any view on this question.

DISCUSSION

The initial, and perhaps most surprising, finding in this survey had to do with the fact that many child and adolescent psychiatrists acknowledged limited or no experience in dealing with homosexual adolescents, a finding which by itself deserved attention and raised several questions.

First, focusing on the adolescents themselves, it could be questioned whether or not they were actually seeking help. Refusal of mental health care is a common reaction among teenagers, partly because of denial, confidentiality issues, and the fear of being labeled "crazy." One could speculate that homosexual adolescents feel even more threatened when considering the option of seeing a psychiatrist. On the other hand, homosexual adolescents may not be connecting with the psychiatrists because a disproportionately high number of them commit suicide before doing so. This frightening proposition is not backed by known statistical data, but is suggested by the results of this survey and will be discussed later. Another possibility may be that homosexual adolescents, more than their heterosexual counterparts, are better adjusted and consequently require less professional help.

None of the survey respondents mentioned this possibility. Evidence, although indirect, suggested that homosexual and heterosexual adults are indistinguishable on the basis of standard measures of psychopathology. Non-patient comparison studies did not document any significant differences (Boyer, 1981); however, extrapolating this finding to the adolescent age group was not based on known research. Random sampling did not seem to have been a problem in regards to the experts. However, it is possible that some may have had practices restricted to a certain group of patients. Yet the magnitude of their lack of exposure to the studied group suggested that they either did not recognize or did not want to treat these patients. Homophobia, or fear of homosexuality, which is pervasive to many aspects of social, religious, and private life, is also present in the psychiatric community and may account for this finding. In fact, some respondents implied this through their written comments like: "Many therapists appear to have biases and areas of sexuality not fully worked through"; "Despite attempts to make it seem to the contrary, I feel that homosexuality is ego-dystonic"; "homophobic introjects are almost inevitable." Countering this argument was a study of adolescent drug users in a residential treatment center which did not show disabling countertransference difficulties that led to the "systematic exclusion" of the homosexual patients (Wellisch, DeAngelis, & Paternite, 1981). This report, however, included professionals from varying disciplines, not just psychiatry. Another significant finding in this survey was that suicidal risk and severity of attempts were considered to be higher by many psychiatrists. Although this opinion was not shared by all, the argument that homosexual adolescents have special circumstances should be further discussed.

It is during adolescence that choices about sexual orientation are thought to be made. Critical factors affecting sexual orientation cannot be identified. Failed heterosexual attempts, rejections, competitiveness, family problems, and jealousy, have all been suspected to play a role. One's homosexual self-awareness usually begins in adolescence, and with it one often has to contend with social disapproval (Malyon, 1981). Although homosexual fantasies and behavior do not always predict adult homosexual object choice, sexual orientation seems to be established in adolescence or even earlier. Still, homosexual thought, regardless of further adult sexual choices, can be overwhelming to any teenager. Malyon (1981) described three possible modes of adaptation in adolescence: repression of sexual desire, suppression of homosexual impulses in favor of heterosexual or asexual orientation, or a homosexual disclosure. All three coping mechanisms have associated problems with the potential for major disruption, dissatisfaction, and alienation. Homosexuality remains a stigma which, by itself, can discredit all other aspects of a person's identity (Martin, 1982). Homosexually oriented adolescents often feel despised, the reason why many of them will decide to "hide," and why they feel isolated from family, peers, groups, and religions.

Similarly, Troiden (1979) described a four-stage model for the attainment of "gay identity." Starting in early adolescence, teenagers become sensitized to their sexual orientation. Then follows a stage of "dissociation" during which they question and sometimes reject the negative social implications of their orientation. They then "come out," and finally are able to fuse their emotionality and sexuality in a harmonious way. For adolescents, all these stages can be difficult to cross. Should the struggles be too overwhelming, then depression and suicide become more likely. In many cases, homo-erotic drives in adolescence remain ego-dystonic and cause disorganization, self-hate, and identity confusion (Malyon, 1982). Low self-esteem, depression, denial, suppression, and compartmentalization are only a few of the defenses used by the adolescents as reported by Malyon (1982) and identified by our respondents.

Homosexual adolescents usually do not have access to gay or lesbian communities since most such communities are adult-oriented (Malyon, 1981). One respondent wrote: "There is so little availability of adult homosexuality role-modeling that is positive, so little open to peer support." This sense of alienation sometimes can push adolescents into casual sexual contacts which may foster the belief that their orientation is deviant and reinforce their sense of worthlessness (Martin, 1982). The depersonalization of the sexual encounters can also lead to self-hatred or projection of hatred to the sexual partner or, on the other hand, to a sudden and false sense of intimacy (Martin, 1982). Homosexual adolescents who have few constructive role models may, therefore, have the most difficulty with identity formation. According to Erikson (1963), identity formation is the most important developmental task in adolescence. From it will develop peer-group interactions and acceptance, with a resulting further consolidation of self-concept and autonomy. Sexual nonconformity can result in total rejection by the peer group. Fragmentation in identity formation can ensue, extending the "adolescing" process for a long period (Malyon, 1982). Yet Malyon reminds us, "No two people function in exactly the same developmental context. Thus not every homosexual becomes symptomatic" (p. 62). The socialization of the homosexual adolescent invariably involves the internalization of some homophobic values "which contaminates the process of adolescent identity formation" (p. 60). These issues were mirrored in the responses of those who completed the questionnaire.

The more liberal social climate of recent decades has encouraged many adolescents to be more open about their homosexuality. A few, however, cannot recognize or accept their sexual orientation and are not capable or willing to reach a satisfactory compromise. These are the ones who may experience diverse psychic conflicts which often manifest as depression, impulsive self-destructiveness (Hunt, 1978), or drug and alcohol abuse (McKenry, 1983; Gonzalez, 1979).

CONCLUSION

Teenage suicide is a major public health problem which has a number of causes. Likewise, homosexuality is thought to have a number of causes. This paper is not trying to minimize or oversimplify the issues. Yet, although homosexuality was "depathologized" in 1973 by the American Psychiatric Association, social attitudes, myths, and stereotypes are slow to change (Malyon, 1981).

Results from this survey suggested that many psychiatrists were not working with homosexual adolescents; thus, the existence of homophobia in the psychiatric profession has to be considered (Steinhorn, 1979). The majority of the respondents, however, agreed that these teenagers were at higher risk for suicide and that their gestures were more severe. Suicidal gestures were thought to be desperate or unconscious pleas for help from adolescents struggling with their sexual orientation. Some homosexual adolescents may see other mental health professionals besides psychiatrists. A study involving these other experts might assist in elucidating some of the questions raised in this report.

Suicide attempts among homosexual adolescents represent maladaptive ways to deal with a poorly understood and widely rejected sexual orientation. Adolescents who face society's negative pressures, whether from family, peers, or other groups may well experience more acutely their conflicting impulses, needs, and desires. These conflicts may generate a series of negative responses, including low self-esteem, loneliness, feelings of worthlessness, rejection, and shame, all possibly culminating into depressive symptoms and suicidal gestures.

REFERENCES

Boyer, R. (1981). *Homosexuality and American psychiatry: The politics of diagnosis.* New York: Basic Books.

Erikson, E. (1963). *Childhood and society* (2nd ed.). New York: W.W. Norton.

Gonzalez, R.M. (1979). Hallucinogenic dependency during adolescence as a defense against homosexual fantasies: A re-enactment of the first separation-individuation phase in the course of treatment. *Journal of Youth and Adolescence, 8*(1), 63–71.

Holinger, P.C. (1978). Adolescent suicide: An epidemiological study of recent trends. *American Journal of Psychiatry, 135,* 745–756.

Holinger, P.C., and Offer, D. (1982). Prediction of adolescent suicide: A population model. *American Journal of Psychiatry, 139,* 302–306.

Hunt, S.P. (1978). Homosexuality from a contemporary perspective. *Connecticut Medicine, 42,* 105–108.

McKenry, P.C. (1983). The role of drugs in adolescent suicide attempts. *Suicide and Life-Threatening Behavior, 13,* 166–175.

Malyon, A.K. (1981). The homosexual adolescent: Developmental issues and social bias. *Child Welfare, 60,* 321–330.

Malyon, A.K. (1982). Biphasic aspects of homosexual identity formation. *Psychotherapy: Theory, Research and Practice, 19,* 335–340.

Malyon, A.K. (1982). Psychotherapeutic implications of internalized homophobia in gay men. In J. Gonsiorek (Ed.), *Homosexuality and psychotherapy* (pp. 59–69). New York: Haworth Press.

Martin, D.A. (1982). Learning to hide: The socialization of the gay adolescent. In Feinstein, Looney, Schwartzberg, and Sorosky (Eds.), *Adolescent psychiatry* (Vol. 10, pp. 52–65). Chicago: University of Chicago Press.

Otto, U. (1972). Suicidal acts by children and adolescents. *Acta Psychiatrica Scandinavica* (Suppl. 233).

Steinhorn, A.I. (1979). Lesbian adolescents in residential treatment. *Social Casework: Journal of Contemporary Social Work, 60,* 494–498.

Troiden, R.R. (1979). Becoming homosexual: A model of gay identity acquisition. *Psychiatry, 42,* 362–373.

Wellisch, D.K., DeAngelis, G.G., and Paternite, C. (1981). A study of therapy of homosexual adolescent drug users in a residential treatment setting. *Adolescence, 16*(63), 698–700.

Williams, C., and Lyons, C.M. (1976). Family interactions and adolescent suicidal behavior: A preliminary investigation. *Australia and New Zealand Journal of Psychiatry, 10,* 243–252.

Violence against Lesbian and Gay Male Youths

JOYCE HUNTER
Hetrick-Martin Institute

From *Journal of Interpersonal Violence*, 5(3)
(September 1990), 295–300.

ABSTRACT: *This article documents the incidence of violent assaults toward lesbian and gay male youths, and those youths' suicidal behavior. Data were obtained by reviewing charts for the first 500 youths seeking services in 1988 at the Hetrick-Martin Institute, a community-based agency serving lesbian and gay male adolescents in New York City. The adolescents, who ranged in age from 14 to 21 years, were predominantly minority (35% Black, 46% Latino) and typically were referred by peers, media, schools, and emergency shelters. Of the youths, 41% in the sample reported having suffered violence from families, peers, or strangers; 46% of that violence was gay-related. These reports of violence occurred in conjunction with a high rate of suicide attempts: 41% of the girls and 34% of the boys who experienced violent assaults reported having attempted suicide. These alarming rates indicate the need for more systematic monitoring of violence toward and suicidal behavior among lesbian and gay male youths.*

Compared to adults, adolescents are disproportionately the victims of violent crime (Select Committee on Children, Youth, and Families,

1989). This violence is often targeted at subgroups of youths. Minority youths, for example, are at greater risk of violent and discriminatory behavior than are White youths. Mont-Reynaud, Ritter, and Chen (1990) found that 69% of Black youths and 54% of Latino youths enrolled in high schools have experienced discrimination, compared to 30% of White youths. Differences between minorities and Whites were even greater when frequent discrimination was examined: only 6% of Whites, but 28% of Blacks and 25% of Latinos experienced frequent discrimination.

Gay male and lesbian youths are another group believed to experience frequent violence, especially as a result of increasing societal homophobia in response to the AIDS epidemic (Berrill, 1990; Finn & McNeil, 1987; Gutis, 1989; Martin, 1988). In a survey of 2,823 junior- and senior-high school students, for example, the New York State Governor's Task Force on Bias-Related Violence found respondents to be not only negatively biased toward gay persons, but "sometimes viciously and with threats of violence" (DeStefano, 1988, p.7). These biases frequently are expressed in harassment and assault of gay- and lesbian-identified students (e.g., Berrill, 1990). Such victimization has many consequences, including truancy and dropping out of school (Hunter & Schaecher, 1990). Violence toward youths also is believed to be associated with violence toward oneself, manifested in the form of suicidal behavior (Gibson, 1989; Hunter & Schaecher, 1990).

Although accounts of gay bashing have increased in the popular press (Rotheram-Borus, Rosario, & Koopman, 1991), few data are available to document the incidence of such attacks against minority youths. Documentation of suicidal ideation and suicide attempts among minority youths also is needed. The goal of the present article, therefore, is to document the frequency of violent attacks and suicidal behaviors reported by a sample of self-identifying lesbian and gay male youths who are also predominantly Black or Latino.

METHOD

Site

The Hetrick-Martin Institute is a community-based agency in New York City that provides a range of services targeting lesbian and gay male teenagers and their families. Youths who seek services at the agency are predominantly minority (35% Black, 46% Latino, with the remaining 19% White, Asian, or mixed), ranging in age from 14 to 21 years (M = 16.8 years). Typically, they are referred by peers, media, schools or emergency shelters. Approximately 80% of those seeking services are male, and 20% are female. Most youths self-identify as homosexual (67%), with the remainder reporting themselves to be bisexual (26%) or unsure about their sexual orientation (7%).

The Institute has six major service components, serving more than 1,000 youths per year: clinical counseling services, a street outreach program, the Harvey Milk High School, an after-school drop-in center program, educational services, and an HIV/health care program. The present study is based on reports from all youths being seen at the Institute except those in the street outreach program.[1]

Procedure

Data for the present article were obtained from the charts of the first 500 youth seeking services at the agency beginning January 1, 1988 (this included charts through approximately November, 1988). Each chart contains information collected during an initial intake interview that lasts from 90 minutes to 2 hours and is conducted with every youth presenting at the agency. This interview includes assessment of demographic information (age, sex, race, sexual orientation, living situation, sources of financial support, religion), status of current psychosocial adjustment (including relations to family, peers, school, and the legal system), sexual abuse, problem behaviors, sexual and drug risk behaviors, health status, and knowledge of HIV and HIV risk.

Of particular relevance to the present article, information is gathered on violence experienced by the youth (physical assaults), its source (family, peers, strangers), and whether it was gay-related or not. Additionally, suicidal behavior is documented both in terms of suicidal ideation (thinking about suicide for more than three days in one week) and actual suicide attempts.

The six members of the clinical staff at the agency were trained to code each chart for the presence or absence of violent physical assaults and the type (anti-gay or not) and source of the violence, as well as the presence or absence of suicidal ideation and attempts. To provide qualitative descriptions of the reports contained in the intake interviews, each counselor wrote a short case report and presented it in group supervision. Two typical cases have been selected for presentation here.

RESULTS

Forty percent (201 of 500) of youths reported that they had experiences violent physical attacks. The youths reporting violence did not differ significantly from the general sample of youths seeking services at the Hetrick-Martin Institute. Their mean age was 17.1; 21% of them were female; 42% were Black, 40% Latino, 16% White, and 2% other. Of those reporting violent physical assaults, 46% reported that the assault was gay-related; 61% of the gay-related violence occurred in the family. Suicidal ideation was found among 44% of those experiencing violent assaults; 41% of the girls and 34% of the boys reporting violent assaults had tried to kill themselves.

A description of two typical cases illustrates the psychological pain associated with violent attacks. Brian, a 16-year-old Black youth, always knew that he was gay. He reported to his intake counselor that he also knew not to talk about his sexual orientation with family or peers. Because he did not pursue girls, a friend asked Brian about his sexual preferences. Brian responded honestly that he preferred males. Fearing that his friendship with Brian would lead to his own ostracism by peers, the friend informed others at school that Brian was gay, telling them in a manner that elicited harassment and ridicule toward Brian. Brian was shoved into lockers, ridiculed, and threatened on a daily basis. Over time, this emotional abuse evolved into physical abuse until, one day after school, Brian was attacked by his schoolmates. His home situation was similar. Brian's parents were unable to tolerate or accept his sexual orientation. His father taunted Brian and their arguments intensified until their relationship was characterized solely by abuse and ridicule. Brian attempted suicide several times before hearing about the Hetrick-Martin Institute and transferring to Harvey Milk High School.

Anna, an 18-year-old Latina, was living in a group home when coming to Hetrick-Martin. Her parents had filed a PINS petition (Persons in Need of Supervision), requesting Anna's placement due to her sexual orientation. When Anna first told her parents that she was lesbian, they felt angry and guilty; they almost filed for divorce, each blaming the other for their daughter's homosexuality. With counseling, they chose not to divorce but to place Anna. She was angry and frequently became involved in arguments and fights, first at school and then in her several foster care and group home placements. Her anger was linked to insults and harassment for being lesbian. This harassment was invisible to the group home counselor, who saw only Anna's angry response and perceived her as victimizing the other youths. Only when Anna attempted suicide did the counselor begin to see her victimization by the other residents. Referring Anna to the Hetrick-Martin Institute was a difficult and long-deliberated decision for the counselor, and a relief for Anna.

DISCUSSION

The chart review revealed that 40% of youths had been violently assaulted; 46% of those assaults were gay-related. Many of the violent incidents occurred at home. Suicide attempts were frequent among members of the group. Due to the limitations in the data, it remains unclear whether suicidal behavior was as common among youths who had not been victims of violence as among those who had been assaulted. Furthermore, it is unclear how often strangers perpetrated violence on gay-identified youths; such violence, however, is common among family members. These questions should be addressed in future research.

Our documentation was limited to physical attacks. Emotional and verbal abuse are probably even more common than physical violence. As revealed by the case vignettes and interviews conducted with clinicians at the agency, physical attacks typically were preceded by an escalating sequence of emotional abuse, name-calling, verbal attacks, and threats of violence.

The case vignettes demonstrate that at the root of violence toward lesbians and gay males are societal attitudes and discriminatory practices. The youths in this study were minority, working class, *and* homosexual. Many of these youths belong to at least three risk groups. Therefore, these youths are typically recipients of societal racism, sexism, and homophobia, with unusually stressful lives (Hunter & Schaecher, 1987; Rotheram-Borus et al., 1991). In addition, because adolescent suicide has increased threefold in the last 10 years (Fisher & Shaffer, 1990), simply being young constitutes another risk factor for suicide. These youths thus comprise one of the highest risk groups for adolescent suicide, higher even than runaway and pregnant teens (Rotheram-Borus et al., 1991). Future research should attempt to replicate the finding of high rates of suicide attempts among gay youths. Researchers also must expand their focus to include additional risk behaviors that may reflect youths' reaction to their victimization by society. Black gay youths, for example, may be more inclined to provoke others to kill them rather than to commit suicide; such victim-precipitated homicide may mask the frequency of suicide in this group (Myers, 1989).

Lesbian and gay male youths are an invisible population. Many do not share their sexual orientation with family, friends, or peers because they fear rejection and violence. Consequently, documenting violence toward and suicide among them is difficult. Yet the data reported here indicate the need to develop responses to their victimization.

Bias-related violence against students in school, for example, needs to be documented and eliminated. School administrators, teachers, social workers, and counselors need to be trained to confront homophobia, counsel victims of bias-related violence, and demystify homosexuality (see Berrill & Herek, 1990). In New York City, the Harvey Milk School was created as a haven for youths who self-identify as lesbian and gay. Ultimately, all schools must provide a safe environment in which children learn tolerance and acceptance of differences. Only when all youths can freely pursue their academic goals in traditional schools can we as a culture claim to be fostering true humanity toward other people.

NOTES

This article was completed with help from the staff at the Hetrick-Martin Institute, Jan Baer, A. Damien Martin, Robert Schaecher, Mary Jane Rotheram, and through the generous sharing of the many lesbian and gay male youths served by the institute.

1. The street outreach program consists of homeless youths who are more likely than others to suffer violence due to conditions of life on the street and involvement with prostitution and drugs. These homeless youths are so different from the general lesbian and gay male teenage population in the New York metropolitan

area that data concerning them will be reported elsewhere. Most of those youths not in the street outreach program (80%) live at home.

REFERENCES

Berrill, K.T. (1990). Describing the problem: Anti-gay violence and victimization in the U.S. — An overview. *Journal of Interpersonal Violence, 5*(3), 274–294.

Berrill, K.T., and Herek, G.M. (1990). Violence against lesbians and gay men: An introduction. *Journal of Interpersonal Violence, 5*(3), 269–273.

DeStefano, A.M. (1988, May 10). NY teens antigay, poll finds. *Newsday,* pp. 7, 21.

Finn, P., and McNeil, T. (1987, October 7). *The response of the criminal justice system to bias crime: An exploratory review.* Contract report submitted to the National Institute of Justice, U.S. Department of Justice.

Fisher, P., and Shaffer D. (1990). Facts about suicide: A review of national mortality statistics and records. In M.J. Rotheram-Borus, J. Bradley, and N. Obolensky (Eds.), *Planning to live: Evaluating and treating suicidal teens in community settings.* Tulsa: University of Oklahoma Press.

Gibson, P. (1989). Gay male and lesbian youth suicide. In M.R. Feinleib (Ed.), *Report to the Secretary's Task Force on Youth Suicide: Vol. 3. Prevention and interventions in youth suicide* (pp. 110–142). Washington, DC: U.S. Department of Health and Human Services.

Gutis, P. (1989, June 8). Attacks on U.S. homosexuals held alarmingly widespread. *New York Times.*

Hunter, J., and Schaecher, R. (1987). Stresses on lesbian and gay adolescents in schools. *Social Work in Education, 9*(3): 180–190.

Hunter, J., and Schaecher, R. (1990). Gay and lesbian youths. In M.J. Rotheram-Borus, J. Bradley, and N. Obolensky (Eds.), *Planning to live: Evaluating and treating suicidal teens in community settings* (pp. 297–317). Tulsa: University of Oklahoma Press.

Martin, D. (1988, September 1). Young, gay — And afraid. *New York Times,* p. A-33.

Myers, H.F. (1989). Urban stress and mental health in Black youths: An epidemiological and conceptual update. In R. Jones (Ed.), *Black adolescents* (pp. 123–152). Berkeley, CA: Cobb & Henry.

Mont-Reynaud, R., Ritter, P., and Chen, Z. (1990, March). *Correlates of perceived discrimination among minority and majority youth in the Dornbush-Steinberg data set.* Paper presented at the biannual meeting of the Society for Research on Adolescence, Atlanta, GA.

Rotheram-Borus, M.J., Rosario, M., and Koopman, C. (1991). Minority youths at high risk: Gay males and runaways. In S. Gore and M.E. Colten (Eds.), *Adolescent stress: Causes and consequences* (pp. 181–200). New York: Aldine.

Select Committee on Children, Youth, and Families, U.S. House of Representatives. (1989). *Down these mean streets: Violence by and against America's children.* Washington, DC: U.S. Government Printing Office.

Suicidal Behavior in Adolescent and Young Adult Gay Men

STEPHEN G. SCHNEIDER, Ph.D.
Suicide Prevention Center of the Family Services of Los Angeles

NORMAN L. FARBEROW, Ph.D.
Suicide Prevention Center of the Family Services of Los Angeles

and GABRIEL N. KRUKS
Los Angeles Gay and Lesbian Community Services Center

From *Suicide and Life-Threatening Behavior, 19*(4)
(Winter 1989), 381–394.

ABSTRACT: *The relationship of homosexuality to suicidal behavior was explored by questionnaire responses from 52 men in gay-and-lesbian college organizations and 56 men in gay rap groups. A family background of alcoholism and physical abuse, social supports perceived as rejecting of homosexuality, and no religious affiliation were associated with a history of suicide ideation, reported by 55% of the participants. Racial/ethnic minorities tended to be overrepresented among suicidal as compared to nonsuicidal gay men. Suicide attempts, reported by 20% of the sample, were most often associated with intrapersonal distress, and occurred most often while individuals were "closeted" and/or in the context of recent rejection for being homosexual. Nearly all attempters were aware of their homosexual feelings, but had not yet established a "positive gay identity" at the time of their first suicide attempt. Suicidal behavior in gay youths may be the product both of familial factors that predispose youths to suicidal behavior, and of social and intrapersonal stressors involved in coming to terms with an emerging homosexual identity.*

This study examines suicidal ideation and attempts in self-identified gay youths attending supportive and social college and community groups. The relationship of suicidal behavior to the stressors peculiar to gay youths has been little explored by empirical research; much of what is known about the subject is based on clinical accounts and theoretical speculation.

Although homosexuality itself is no longer considered to be psychopathological (American Psychiatric Association, 1980), psychosocial stressors associated with establishing a gay identity and life style (as a member of a stigmatized minority) have been cited as factors contributing to a higher prevalence of alcoholism (Fitfield, 1975; Lohrenz, Connelly, Coyne, & Spare, 1978; Nardi, 1982) and suicidal behavior in both gay adults (e.g., Bell & Weinberg, 1978; Climent, Ervin, Rollins, Plutchik, & Batinelli, 1977; Rofes, 1983; Saghir & Robins, 1973; Saghir, Robins, Walbran, & Gentry, 1970) and adolescents (Harry, 1983, 1986; Kremer & Rifkin, 1969; Remafedi, 1987a, 1978b; Roesler & Deisher, 1972).

Gay persons have been described as experiencing psychosocial difficulties because of (1) alienation and disenfranchisement from the resources and assistance society ordinarily provides in the face of life stressors (Saunders & Valente, 1987); (2) hostile attitudes and actions directed against gay people (Herek, 1986; Laren, Reed, & Hoffman, 1980; Remafedi, 1987b); and (3) distress that is the result of internalized negative attitudes toward one's own homosexuality (Malyon, 1982).

Remafedi (1987a, 1987b) found that half of the suicide attempts in his study of 29 gay youths were directly related to conflicts about sexual orientation, especially after self-identification as a homosexual. Roesler and Deisher (1972) found the period between first homosexual experience and self-designation as a homosexual to be extremely difficult emotionally; 31% of their 60 subjects had made suicide attempts.

The suicide attempt rates observed in these studies of gay youths are higher than the suicide attempt rates reported in studies of nonclinical, general youth populations. Among high school students, rates range from 8.4% (Smith & Crawford, 1986) to 13% (Ross, 1986); a rate of 15% has been reported among college students (Mishara, Baker, & Mishara, 1976).

Few studies have looked at the relationship of homosexuality-related stress to suicidal behavior in samples not specifically identified as gay. One exception is a study by Carmen and Blaine (1970), who found 44 male attempters among all Harvard students during 1963 through 1967: 27% of these had engaged in homosexual activities. It was not possible, however, to determine the specific role of homo-sexuality-related stress in the suicide attempts of these men. Harry's (1983, 1986) study of gender-role nonconformity among males indi-cated that suicide attempts were significantly associated primarily with being an adolescent loner, with childhood sex-role noncon-formity, and with homosexuality, especially with negative feelings about one's incipient homosexuality.

Some of the family factors predisposing among youths in general to suicide have been identified as follows: family environments that are aggressive, chaotic, and unstable (Adam, 1986; Adam, Bouckoms, & Streiner, 1982; Adam, Lohrenz, & Harper, 1982); paternal alcohol and drug use (Garfinkel, Froese, & Hood, 1982); and physical abuse (Green, 1978). A survey of California youths found that those report-ing suicidal events associated them most often with severe family problems and disturbed family relationships (Farberow, Litman, & Nelson, 1987).

A major hypothesis in this study was that gay youths who reported serious suicidal thoughts and/or suicide attempts during adolescence would come from families with greater dysfunction than gay youths who did not report suicidal thoughts/attempts. Equally important, it was expected that suicidal gay youths would report more stressful social relationships and less support in regard to an emerging homo-sexual orientation than gay youths who did not report suicidal thoughts or attempts.

METHOD

Subjects

Subjects consisted of two groups of self-identified gay men be-tween 16 and 24 years of age. One group (gay college, or GC; *n* = 52) was drawn from gay-and-lesbian student organizations from 14 Los Angeles area colleges. A second group (gay rap group, or GRG; $n = 56$) was drawn from rap groups conducted by the local gay-and-lesbian community center. Participation was voluntary. Subjects were judged by their respective group leaders to be representative of all persons attending meetings, and over 90% of those present when questionnaires were distributed participated.

Materials

Subjects completed a questionnaire requesting information on suicidal thoughts and feelings, with items specifically focused on fleeting thoughts of suicide, serious thoughts of suicide, and serious consideration of acting on the suicidal thoughts. Each item was rated on a Likert-type 7-point scale (from "never" to "chronically") over three time periods: (1) before age 14; (2) age 14 and after; and (3) the last 6 months. Subjects also indicated the number of suicidal plans and attempts they had made for each time period. Information was obtained on the age at which each attempt had occurred, accompanying thoughts and feelings, and the treatment received (if any).

Demographic data were collected, as well as information on early home and family experiences (e.g., familial substance abuse, physical and sexual abuse, and suicidal behavior). Levels of current social support (e.g., from family, peers, groups, etc.) were measured, along with the degree to which each source accepted or rejected the subject's sexual orientation. Subjects were also asked to report the age at which they (1) reached critical stages (McDonald, 1982) in the process of "coming out" and (2) "came out" to various relationships, and the degree of acceptance or rejection they received on "coming out."

Subjects were given an informed consent form to sign, an assurance of confidentiality, and the phone number of a 24-hour suicide hotline.

Results

Statistical methods employed were chi-squared tests, t tests, Fisher's exact tests, and, using general linear models, analyses of variance and least-squares means (the latter for simple effects analyses) (Marascuilo & Levin, 1983; SAS Institute, 1985; Winer, 1971).

The GC and GRC men were combined to form one group for study. The two groups did not significantly differ in religion, race, length of longest intimate relationship, or percentage reporting suicide attempts (GC, 19%; GRC, 23%) or suicidality (defined below) (GC, 52%; GRC, 59%). The GC men were slightly, though significantly, older (M = 21.2 years) than the GRG men (M = 20.0 years), ($p < .01$). Combining the two groups was considered acceptable.

Demographic and Suicide Characteristics of the Combined Group

Table 1 shows the demographic characteristics of the suicidal (S; n = 59) and nonsuicidal (NS; n = 49) subjects, and of the combined group. "Suicidal" was defined by a reported history of either serious suicidal thoughts occasionally, serious consideration of a suicidal action occasionally, the formation of a suicide plan, or a suicide attempt.

The S and NS gay men did not differ in age, education, or employment status. Significantly more of the S (31%) than of the NS (14%) gay men reported no religious affiliation ($p < .05$). No other religious differences emerged. A trend indicated that racial/ethnic minorities constituted more of the S group (35.6%) than of the NS group (22.5%) ($p < .14$). In another trend, more of the S (32%) than of the NS (20%) gay men reported never having had an intimate partner ($p < .18$).

Among the early familial events and experiences studied, those reported rarely (by fewer than 5% of subjects) were parental death and drug use; sibling intravenous drug use; and familial sexual abuse and suicide. More frequently reported events were divorce; familial alcoholism; sibling nonintravenous drug use; and familial physical abuse and suicide attempts. Of all these indicators of familial dysfunction, group differences reached significance only for father's alcoholism: 25.4% of the S versus 8.2% of the NS gay men reported alcoholic fathers ($p < .05$). Marked trends were found for familial physical abuse (S, 18.6%; NS, 6.1%; $p < .054$) and familial suicide attempts (S, 20.3%; NS, 8.2%; $p < .08$).

Social Supports of Recently Suicidal and Recently Nonsuicidal Gay Men

Social support ratings over the last 6 months were compared for recently (over last 6 months) S (n = 28) and NS (n = 80) gay men.

TABLE 1. Characteristics of Suicidal and Nonsuicidal Gay Men

Variables	Nonsuicidal (n=49)		Suicidal (n=59)		Combined (n=108)	
	Mean	(SD)	Mean	(SD)	Mean	(SD)
Age	20.8	(2.1)	20.4	(2.1)	20.6	(2.1)
	Number	(%)	Number	(%)	Number	(%)
Religion						
Protestant	14	(28.6)	15	(25.4)	29	(26.8)
Catholic	21	(42.9)	21	(35.6)	42	(38.9)
Jewish	6	(12.2)	4	(6.8)	10	(9.3)
Other	1	(2.0)	1	(1.7)	2	(1.9)
No Religion[a]	7	(14.3)	18	(30.5)	25	(23.1)
Race						
White	38	(77.5)	38	(64.4)	76	(70.4)
Minority[b]	11	(22.5)	21	(35.6)	32	(29.6)
Black	2	(4.1)	2	(3.4)	4	(3.7)
Pacific/Asian	1	(2.0)	4	(6.8)	5	(4.6)
Latino	5	(10.2)	11	(18.6)	16	(14.8)
Multiple/other	3	(6.1)	4	(6.8)	7	(6.5)
Longest intimate relationship						
None[c]	10	(20.4)	19	(32.2)	29	(26.8)
< 2 years	32	(65.3)	36	(61.0)	68	(63.0)
> 2 years	7	(14.3)	4	(6.8)	11	(10.2)
Father alcoholic[d]						
No	45	(91.8)	44	(74.6)	89	(82.4)
Yes	4	(8.2)	15	(25.4)	19	(17.6)

a. Subjects not indicating a religion significantly overrepresented in the suicidal group compared to all subjects indicating some religious affiliation (p < .05).
b. Trend for minority overrepresentation in the suicidal group (p < .14).
c. Trend for overrepresentation of those with no history of an intimate relationship among suicidal group (p < .18).
d. Difference between suicidal and nonsuicidal groups (p < .02).

Three variables were compared: "number," the total number of supports reported from all sources; "importance," the importance of each support, summed across all sources; and "dependency," the dependency felt on each support, summed across all sources. No significant differences appeared between the recently S and NS gay men on number (M = 32.9 vs. M = 28.8); importance (M = 27.5 vs. M = 27.8); or dependency (M = 24.0 vs. M = 24.6), respectively.

Subjects also rated (on a 7-point scale) the degree to which each social support had accepted or rejected their homosexuality in the last 6 months. Each support was considered either "accepting" (rated <5); "rejecting" (rated >4); or "unaware" (rated as such). By means of three mixed-model analyses of variance, differences between the recently S and NS gay men (group) in accepting, rejecting, or unaware (condition) relationships were explored separately for number, importance, and dependency (dependent measures). In keeping with the hypotheses of this study, the focus below is on significant between-group differences.

For importance, a significant main effect of condition, F (2, 318) = 31.38, $p <$ .0001, and interaction, F (2, 318) = 5.52, $p <$ .01, emerged. Between-group differences (using least-squares means) indicated that the recently S gay men rated rejecting social supports as significantly more important (S, M = 5.89; NS, M = 2.10; $p <$ .02); recently NS gay men rated unaware social supports as significantly more important (NS, M = 13.73; S, M = 9.93; $p <$ .02). There were no group differences in the rated importance of accepting social supports (S, M = 11.71; NS, M = 11.98).

For dependency, a significant main effect of condition, F (2, 318) = 39.79, $p <$ .0001, and interaction, F (2, 318) = 3.28, $p <$ .04, emerged. Least-squares means comparisons found the following trends: Recently S gay men depended more on rejecting social supports (S, M = 4.18; NS, M = 1.65; $p <$ .09); recently NS gay men depended more on unaware social supports (NS, M = 11.06; S, M = 8.32; $p <$ .06). There were no group differences in the rated dependence on accepting social supports (S, M = 11.50; NS, M = 11.85).

For number, only the main effect of condition was significant, F (2, 318) = 33.23, $p <$ .0001. Post hoc analyses revealed that both groups identified nearly equal numbers of accepting (S, M = 16.92; NS, M = 16.31) and unaware (S, M = 9.29; NS, M = 10.03) social supports; however, recently S gay men identified significantly more rejecting social supports (S, M = 6.68; NS, M = 2.42; $p <$ .05).

Characteristics of Gay Suicide Attempters

Twenty-two participants reported suicide attempts. The mean age at the time of the first suicide attempt was 16.3 years; the youngest age at first attempt was 12. Twelve attempters had made a single attempt;

TABLE 2. Feelings Reported by Suicide-Attempting Gay Men (n =21) at the Time of the First Attempt

Statement	Mean	(SD)
Felt no hope for the future	1.7	(1.5)
Experienced painful feelings	2.0	(1.7)
Felt helpless	2.2	(1.8)
Felt worthless or inadequate	2.4	(1.8)
Felt lonely or isolated	2.6	(2.0)
Felt unacceptable to myself	3.0	(2.2)
Intended to die	3.2	(2.4)
Wanted to get back at someone	3.2	(2.4)
Felt unacceptable to others	3.3	(2.4)
Felt angry at another	3.3	(2.6)
Felt hurt by another	3.4	(2.5)
Thought something wrong with or different about me	3.4	(2.5)
Recently broke up with a lover	4.7	(2.8)

Note: Ratings range from 1 = "true" through 7 = "false."

10 reported 2 to 14 attempts. Eleven attempters received no treatment for their first attempt; six received only outpatient psychotherapy; two received some type of medical treatment or hospitalization; and three received both outpatient psychotherapy and medical treatment.

Average ratings of statements describing feelings at the time of the first attempt were shown in Table 2. On a 7-point scale, items rated as mostly true (<3) describe an intrapersonal state (e.g., pain, hopelessness, helplessness, worthlessness, and alienation). Statements rated 3 or 4 (neither true nor false) described mostly an interpersonal state (e.g., anger, revenge, unacceptability to others). The only question rated false (>4) was "I had recently broken up with a lover."

Identity Formation

Table 3 compares the mean ages at which attempters (*n* = 21) and nonsuicidal (*n* = 49) gay men reported having reached critical milestones in the "coming-out" process. Attempters reported being significantly younger when they first were aware of being attracted to members of the same sex (*p* < .01); first labeled their feelings, but not themselves, as homosexual (*p* < .04); first questioned the socially

TABLE 3. Mean Age and Standard Deviation of Gay Suicide Attempters and Nonsuicidal Gay Men at Critical Points of Gay Identity Formation

Stages	Group		Nonsuicidal	
	Suicide attempters			
Awareness of same-sex attractions	8.1	(3.9)***	10.7	(3.6)
	(n=21)	(n=47)		
Understood what the word				
"homosexual" means	12.8	(3.7)	12.5	(2.8)
	(n=21)	(n=49)		
Feelings labeled as homosexual,				
but not self	12.1	(3.3)**	14.1	(3.4)
	(n=18)	(n=44)		
Questioned socially prescribed				
heterosexual identity	13.8	(2.8)*	15.1	(2.3)
	(n=21)	(n=44)		
Sexual activities with members of				
own sex	13.1	(3.6)	14.6	(4.4)
	(n=20)	(n=47)		
Involved in first homosexual				
relationship	16.2	(2.2)***	17.7	(2.3)
	(n=19)	(n=43)		
Considered self homosexual	16.0	(3.2)	16.6	(2.9)
	(n=21)	(n=46)		
Described self as gay; felt good				
about being gay	18.3	(1.6)	18.5	(2.5)
	(n=19)	(n=43)		

*p < .07.   **p < .05.   ***p < .015.

prescribed heterosexual identity (*p* < .065); and first became involved in a homosexual relationship (*p* < .015).

Table 4 shows the number of attempters who reached these critical milestones in "coming out" (McDonald, 1982) either before, at the time of, or after their first attempt. Twenty of the attempters were aware of being attracted to members of their own sex before their first suicide attempt. Yet only two had reached the point at which they described themselves as gay or felt good about their homosexuality before they made their first attempt. One-fourth made their first attempt at about the time when they were questioning their heterosexual identity and/or when they first had sex with same-sex partners.

The attempters (*n* = 21) did not differ from the nonsuicidal gay men (*n* = 49) in the degree of acceptance or rejection they received from key supports on "coming out." However, of the 21 attempters, only 4 had disclosed their sexuality to any key support before their first

TABLE 4. Number and Percentage of Gay Suicide Attempters Who Reported Having Attained Each Stage of Gay Identity Formation, Relative to the Time of Their First Suicide Attempt

	Stage Attained					
	Before attempt		At the time of attempt		After attempt or not attained	
Stage	Number	(%)	Number	(%)	Number	(%)
Awareness of same-sex attractions	20	(95.2)	0	(00.0)	1	(4.8)
Understood what the word "homosexual" means	15	(71.4)	3	(14.3)	3	(14.3)
Feelings labeled as homosexual, but not self	14	(66.7)	2	(9.5)	5	(23.8)
Questioned socially prescribed heterosexual identity	14	(66.7)	5	(23.8)	2	(9.5)
Sexual activities with members of own sex	13	(61.9)	5	(23.8)	3	(14.3)
Involved in first homosexual relationship	7	(33.3)	3	(14.3)	11	(52.4)
Considered self homosexual	8	(38.1)	4	(19.0)	9	(42.9)
Described self as gay; felt good about being gay	2	(9.5)	3	(14.3)	16	(76.2)

attempt. Of eight attempters who were "coming out" shortly before or after their first attempt, six were rejected by at least one key support.

DISCUSSION

The generalizability of results generated from studies of non-normative social groups always presents problems, even when efforts are made to employ representative samples. Thus, our findings may not generalize well beyond "gay youths attending social and supportive college and community groups." Intellectual level and economic status inherent in the two subject groups, as well as unidentified factors that affect the willingness of some to volunteer data on emotionally disturbing experiences, may affect generalizability of these results to all other self-identified gay men.

Given that the subjects sampled were relatively open about their sexuality, the reported level of suicidal ideation and behavior may be an underestimate of what is found in the gay youth population in general (i.e., more "closeted" gay youths may be experiencing greater distress). This sampling bias, however, would be balanced by the possibility that the gay men sampled were more distressed than some gay youths who do not attend supportive groups; the latter may feel less need for group support.

It is worth noting that over 90% of those present at any meeting where participation was solicited did so. Also, gay organizations from 14 Los Angeles area campuses, as well as gay rap groups from two very distinct socioeconomic/geographic communities, were represented. Thus it seems possible to assume that the sample studied is representative, at least, of the population of self-identified gay male youths who attend rap groups and gay college organizations.

With these possible sampling biases acknowledged, the high level of suicide attempts (20%) and of serious suicidal ideation (55%) reported by our participants merits clinical and social concern. A major factor contributing to suicidality here, as expected, overlaps with predictors of suicidality in the general youth population: family dysfunction. In particular, paternal alcoholism was significantly more frequent among suicidal gay youths. Up to 60% of adolescent suicide attempters in other studies have been found to have alcoholic fathers (Garfinkel et al., 1982). A father's alcoholism may have a wide-ranging impact on overall family functioning, and may provide the child/ adolescent with an inadequate model for coping with the world.

Within our sample, post hoc analyses indicated that father's alcoholism was significantly ($p < .003$) associated with familial physical abuse, especially of the mother ($p < .002$) and the subject ($p < .008$). Mother's alcoholism, however, was not associated with familial physical abuse or suicidality. It may be that the physical violence accompanying a father's alcoholism contributes most to the environment out of which a suicidal adolescent emerges. Indeed, *all* of the gay men who reported alcoholic fathers *and* familial physical abuse ($n = 7$) were suicidal.

Significantly more of the suicidal than of the nonsuicidal gay youths sampled reported no religion. These youths may have abandoned their familial religion (a likely event, given religious condemnations of homosexuality), or they may have been raised without any religion. In either case, if religion serves a protective function vis-à-vis youth suicidality in general, such protection may not be readily available to many gay youths, for whom a religious affiliation may be conflictual at best. The impact and function of religion among gay youths (and adults) is little understood, and calls for further investigation.

We observed a trend toward greater suicidal thought among racial/ethnic minority gay men, particularly among Latino gay men, than among white gay men (in contrast to the trend in the general population). Whether particular cultural factors *may* contribute to suicidal thinking and behavior among gay Latinos is beyond the scope of our study. Our small sample of minority men further argues for a cautious interpretation of the results. In general, however, being a stigmatized "minority within a minority" may contribute to suicidality: Gay members of ethnic minorities are often disenfranchised from both mainstream and minority social institutions that normally provide support and psychological protection from distress symptomatology. Future studies of sociocultural factors that may contribute to suicidality among gay persons within particular and across all minority groups are warranted.

In the realm of social support, the data reveal that recently suicidal gay men may (1) have more supports viewed as rejecting of their sexuality, (2) depend more on these supports, and (3) view them as more important. Although there were no group differences in the absolute number of supports to whom gay men remained "closeted," nonsuicidal gay men rated such supports as more important, and rated greater dependence on such supports.

It is of course true that the emotional concomitants of the suicidal period itself can increase alienation from potential supports (e.g., "unaware" supports) and may cause other supports to be seen as rejecting. The effects of *actual* "negative support," however, need to be further explored. Important and needed supports who are rejecting of homosexuality may directly cause distress symptoms, and also may increase alienation from others: Expectancies of further rejection from "unaware" supports may be increased, and overall perceived and real levels of social support may be thereby reduced.

In regard to the relationship between the emergence of homosexuality and suicide attempts, it appears that (1) attempters, compared to nonsuicidal gay youths, reported that they were grappling with their homosexuality earlier in adolescence; (2) at the time of their first attempt, most attempters were aware of their homosexuality, but had not yet felt good about themselves as gay men; (3) first attempts were reported as *intra*personal, rather than as interpersonal, acts (i.e., *not* following romantic breakups, as is often reported in adolescents in general); and (4) most attempters were still "closeted" at the time of their first attempt, and those who were "coming out" experienced rejection. Thus attempts were made during psychologically stressful periods of the "coming-out" process, in relative isolation, or in the fear (or actual experience) of rejection from potential social supports.

In grappling with their homosexuality at an earlier age, attempters would be less well equipped psychologically and socially to cope with sexual feelings. It is important to note that though the nonsuicidal gay youths were "coming out" somewhat later than the attempters, the differences observed were on the order of 1–3 years. Nonsuicidal gay youths were, on average, beginning the process of exploring and expressing their sexuality in early adolescence; this study does not address the psychological effects of developmental delays, common among gay persons, that may move the resolution of normatively adolescent sexual issues into the years of adulthood.

The role of a dysfunctional family in (1) providing inadequate resources with which to cope with homosexuality, or (2) setting the stage for stressful or rejecting relationships, warrants further investigation. It is likely that gay youths from functional families may be more able to mobilize resources (familial and other) with which to cope with the stressors associated with their incipient homosexuality: Their personal relationships may be more supportive, and they may more readily establish intimate relationships with partners (associated in this study with being nonsuicidal). In gay youths from dysfunctional families, it is difficult to determine whether stressful (and possibly suicidogenic) relationships are related to or independent of the youths' homosexuality.

In sum, the present study indicates that (1) family dysfunction, particularly paternal alcoholism and physical abuse, may be characteristic of the backgrounds of those gay male youths most likely to report suicidal ideation in adolescence; (2) suicidal ideation in gay male youths is often accompanied by perceived (or actual) rejection by important and needed social supports for an emerging homosexual identity; and (3) suicide attempts among gay male youths are mostly intrapersonal acts carried out as these adolescents grapple with difficult aspects of an emerging homosexual identity, in basic isolation, or in the context of rejection for being homosexual.

Suicidal behavior in gay male youths may be exacerbated by predisposing familial environments, which ill prepare the youths to cope adequately with the many stressors involved in establishing a supportive homosexual identity during adolescence. The relative contributions of family background and homosexuality-related stressors to suicidal ideation and behavior in gay male youths have yet to be determined.

NOTE

We gratefully acknowledge Charlotte Spitzer, M.F.C.C., whose inspiration, encouragement, and ideas helped initiate and motivate our interest in pursuing this topic. We would also like to thank Nancy Taylor for her assistance in preparing this manuscript. Finally, we thank our subjects, who gave so much of their time and effort in sharing their experiences.

REFERENCES

Adam, K.S. (1986). Early family influences on suicidal behavior. *Annals of the New York Academy of Sciences, 487,* 63–76.

Adam, K.S., Bouckoms, A., and Streiner, D. (1982). Parental loss and family stability in attempted suicide. *Archives of General Psychiatry, 39,* 1081–1085.

Adam, K.S., Lohrenz, J., and Harper, D. (1982). Early parental loss and suicide ideation in university students. *Canadian Journal of Psychiatry, 27,* 275–281.

American Psychiatric Association. (1980). *Diagnostic and statistical manual of mental disorders* (3rd ed.). Washington, DC: Author.

Bell, A.P., and Weinberg, M.S. (1978). *Homosexualities: A study of diversity among men and women.* New York: Simon & Schuster.

Carmen, J., and Blaine, A. (1970). A study of suicide attempts by male and female university students. *International Psychiatric Clinics, 7,* 181–199.

Climent, C.E., Ervin, F.R., Rollins, A., Plutchik, R., and Batinelli, C.J. (1977). Epidemiological studies of female prisoners: IV. Homosexual behavior. *Journal of Nervous and Mental Disease, 164,* 25–29.

Farberow, N.L., Litman, R.E., and Nelson, F. (1987). *Suicidal behaviors among California youth.* Paper presented at the Joint Congress of the American Association of Suicidology/International Association of Suicide Prevention, San Francisco.

Fifield, L. (1975). *On my way to nowhere: Alienated, isolated, drunk.* Los Angeles: Gay Community Services Center and Department of Health Services.

Garfinkel, B.D., Froese, A., and Hood, J. (1982). Suicide attempts in children and adolescents. *American Journal of Psychiatry, 140,* 543–547.

Green, A.H. (1978). Self-destructive behavior in battered children. *American Journal of Psychiatry, 135,* 579–582.

Harry, J. (1983). Parasuicide, gender, and gender deviance. *Journal of Health and Social Behavior, 24,* 350–361.

Harry, J. (1986, May). *Adolescent suicide and sexual identity issues.* Paper presented at the Risk Factors in Adolescent Suicide Conference, National Institute of Mental Health, Washington, DC.

Herek, G.M. (1986). On heterosexual masculinity: Some psychical consequences of the social construction of gender and sexuality. *American Behavioral Scientist, 29,* 563–577.

Kremer, M., and Rifkin, A. (1969). The early development of homosexuality: A study of adolescent lesbians. *American Journal of Psychiatry, 126,* 91–96.

Larsen, K.S., Reed, M., and Hoffman, S. (1980). Attitudes of heterosexuals toward homosexuality: A Likert-type scale and construct validity. *Journal of Sex Research, 16,* 245–257.

Lohrenz, L., Connelly, J., Coyne, L., and Spare, K. (1978). Alcohol problems in several Midwestern homosexual communities. *Journal of Studies on Alcohol, 39,* 1959–1963.

McDonald, G.J. (1982). Individual differences in the coming out process for gay men: Implications for theoretical models. *Journal of Homosexuality, 8,* 47–60.

Malyon, A.K. (1982). Psychotherapeutic implications of internalized homophobia in gay men. *Journal of Homosexuality, 7,* 59–70.

Marascuilo, L.A., and Levin, J.R. (1983). *Multivariate statistics in the social sciences: A researcher's guide.* Pacific Grove, CA: Brooks/Cole.

Mishara, B.L., Baker, A.H., and Mishara, T.T. (1976). The frequency of suicide attempts: A retrospective approach applied to college students. *American Journal of Psychiatry, 133:* 841–844.

Nardi, ,.M. (1982). Alcoholism and homosexuality: A theoretical perspective. In T.O. Ziebold and J.E. Mongeon (Eds.), *Alcoholism and sexuality* (pp. 9–25). New York: Haworth Press.

Remafedi, G. (1987a). Male homosexuality: Psychosocial and medical implications. *Pediatrics, 79,* 326–330.

Remafedi, G. (1987b). Adolescent homosexuality: Psychosocial and medical implications. *Pediatrics, 79,* 331–337.

Roesler, T., and Deisher, R.W. (1972). Youthful male homosexuality. *Journal of the American Medical Association, 219,* 1018–1023.

Rofes, E.E. (1983). *"I thought people like that killed themselves": Lesbians, gay men, and suicide.* San Francisco: Grey Fox Press.

Ross, C.P. (1986). Teaching the facts of life and death: Suicide prevention in the schools. In N.L. Farberow, R.E. Litman, and M. Peck (Eds.), *Youth suicide* (pp. 147–169). New York: Springer.

Saghir, M.T., and Robins, E. (1973). *Male and female homosexuality: A comprehensive investigation.* Baltimore: Williams & Wilkins.

Saghir, M.T., Robins, E., Walbran, B., and Gentry, K.S. (1970). Homosexuality: III. Psychiatric disorders and disability in the male homosexual. *American Journal of Psychiatry, 126,* 1079–1086.

SAS Institute. (1985). *SAS user's guide: Statistics, version 5 edition.* Cary, NC: Author.

Saunders, J.M., and Valente, S.M. (1987). Suicide risk among gay men and lesbians: A review. *Death Studies,* 1–23.

Smith, K., and Crawford, S. (1986). Suicidal behavior among "normal" high school students. *Suicide and Life-Threatening Behavior, 16,* 313–325.

Winer, B.J. (1971). *Statistical procedures in experimental design* (2nd ed.). New York: McGraw-Hill.

Risk Factors for Attempted Suicide in Gay and Bisexual Youth

GARY REMAFEDI, M.D., M.P.H.
*Adolescent Health Program, Department of Pediatrics,
University of Minnesota Hospital and Clinic, Minneapolis*

JAMES A. FARROW, M.D.
*Division of Adolescent Medicine, Department of Pediatrics,
University of Washington, Seattle*

and ROBERT W. DEISHER, M.D.
*Division of Adolescent Medicine, Department of Pediatrics,
University of Washington, Seattle*

From *Pediatrics, 87*(6) (June 1991), 869–875.

ABSTRACT: *Studies of human sexuality have noted high rates of suicidality among homosexual youth, but the problem has not been systematically examined. This work was undertaken to identify risk factors for suicide attempts among bisexual and homosexual male youth. Subjects were 137 gay and bisexual males, 14 through 21 years of age, from the upper Midwest and Pacific Northwest. Forty-one subjects (41/137) reported a suicide attempt; and almost half of them described multiple attempts. Twenty-one percent of all attempts resulted in medical or psychiatric admissions. Compared with non-attempters, attempters had more feminine gender roles and adopted a bisexual or homosexual identity at younger ages. Attempters were more likely than peers to report sexual abuse, drug abuse, and arrests for misconduct. The findings parallel previous studies' results and also introduce novel suicide risk factors related to gender noncon-formity and sexual milestones.*

According to most recent statistics, more than 5000 U.S. adolescents and young adults (aged 15 to 24) take their own lives each year.[1] During the past 25 years, suicide rates for young men quadrupled, and self-inflicted death became the second-leading cause of adolescent mortality. These disturbing trends have led to an ongoing search for epidemiological, psychological, and sociological risk factors. Despite considerable progress and new information, the unifying character-istics of young victims are still incompletely understood.[2]

The impact of sexual identity on suicide risk is a relatively un-charted area of research. To date, most surveys of suicide attempters and psychological autopsies of victims have not examined sexual dimensions beyond gender.[3] However, surveys on homosexual popu-lations have raised questions about suicide risk in relation to sexual orientation. An unusual prevalence of suicide attempts and ideation among homosexual persons has surfaced repeatedly as an incidental finding in studies of human sexuality.[4-8]

Forty percent of 5000 homosexual men and women who were surveyed by Jay and Young[4] seriously considered or attempted sui-cide. Bell and Weinberg[5] found that 1000 black and white homosexual men were, respectively, 12 and 3 times more likely than heterosexual men to report suicidal ideation or attempts. The homosexual men were more likely to have made attempts during adolescence than adulthood. Saghir and Robins[6] reported that all suicide attempts in a cohort of homosexual adults occurred during adolescence, often in association with a history of childhood gender atypical behavior or emotional disturbance. In two different studies of homosexual and bisexual adolescents,[7,8] one third of boys reported attempts, and repeat attempts were common.

Two thirds of randomly sampled U.S. psychiatrists[9] believed that the self-injurious acts of homosexual adolescents were more serious and lethal than those of their heterosexual peers. The recent *Report of the Secretary's Task Force on Youth Suicide*[10] projected that gay adolescents were two to three times more likely than peers to attempt suicide, accounting for as many as 30% of completed youth suicides each year. Theoretical risk factors include "coming out" at a young age, gender atypicality, low self-esteem, substance abuse, running away, involvement in prostitution, and other psychosocial morbidities. However, such predictors have not been studied empirically. This work was undertaken to identify risk factors for suicide attempts among gay and bisexual youth, with a broader goal to advance understanding of self-inflicted deaths among adolescents.

SUBJECTS

Subjects were 137 males, between 14 and 21 years of age, who identified themselves as gay (88%) or bisexual (12%). They were recruited during a 1-year period of time (1988) through advertisements in gay publications (30%) and bars (5%), social support groups for gay and lesbian youth (20%) and university students (15%), a youth drop-in center (19%), and referral from peers (11%). None were referred from mental health treatment facilities. Interviews took place in Minneapolis or Seattle. The project was advertised as a study of health issues for gay and bisexual male youth, 21 years of age or younger.

Participants resided in the states of Minnesota (67%), Washington (31%), South Dakota (1%), or Wisconsin (1%). The ethnic/racial composition of the group was 82% white, 13% African-American, 4% Hispanic, and 1% Asian. Other demographic characteristics are summarized in Table 1. Thirty percent of participants (41/137) reported at least one suicide attempt.

METHODS

All participants completed a structured interview regarding demography, education, home, environment, sexuality, and psychosocial history (adapted from a previous study of adolescent homosexuality).[11] Suicide attempts were defined as deliberate acts intended to cause death. Suicide attempts were assessed in interview, using Weisman and Worden's Risk Rescue Rating Scale.[12] When subjects reported multiple attempts, only the latest three were used.

According to Weisman and Worden,[12] the overall seriousness of a suicide attempt is "a balance of calculated factors related to the

TABLE 1. Demographic Characteristics (Means and Percent Frequency Distribution [%F]) of Suicide Attempters and Nonattempters

Variable	Attempters (n=41)	Nonattempters (n=96)
Mean age, y (SD)	19.25 (1.63)	19.83 (1.63)
Mean grade level (SD)	11.58 (1.86)	12.42 (1.98)
Race, %F		
White	76	85
Black, Native American, Hispanic, Asian	24	15
Residence, %F		
Urban	66	71
Suburban/rural	34	29
Interview location, %F		
Minneapolis	59	74
Seattle	42	26
Primary financial support, %F		
Employment (self)	43	55
Parents	35	34
Other	22	11
Religion, %F		
Catholic	20	24
Protestant	24	35
Other*	29	24
None	27	17

*Includes non-Christian faiths or religiosity, without specific affiliation.

degree of irreversible damage and the resources that facilitate or hinder rescue." Weisman and Worden's method rates attempts by degrees of risk and rescuability and provides a composite ratio of risk and rescue factors. "Risk points" correspond to the method of injury, subsequent physical impairment, and the type of medical care that was administered. "Rescue points" are determined by the victim's location, request for help, and rescuer's identity, and the duration of time until discovery. The total risk and rescue points are converted to respec-tive scores, which correspond to intervals on Likert-type scales ranging from "least" to "most" risky or rescuable. When the victims sought help for themselves, their attempts automatically receive a "most rescuable" score. The composite risk-rescue ratio is computed by dividing the risk score by the sum of risk and rescue factors.

All participants also completed (in interview) the Scale for Suicide Ideation,[13] which measures current suicidal intent by scaling various dimensions of self-destructive thoughts and wishes. Four other written instruments were administered. The Bem Sex Role Inventory[14] was used to rate masculinity and femininity and to classify sex-role as feminine, masculine, androgynous (i.e., high masculine/high feminine), or undifferentiated (i.e., low masculine/low feminine). Current levels of depression and hopelessness were respectively measured with the Beck Depression Inventory[15] and the Hopelessness Scale.[16] Finally, personal attitudes toward homosexuality were rated by the Modified Attitudes toward Homosexuality Scale.[17]

Subjects gave verbal and written consent to study procedures. Participation was voluntary and confidential. Completion of procedures required approximately 1.5 hours. Subjects were reimbursed for participation and were given a list of resources for social support and mental health and medical care. Those who indicated active suicidal intent or other acute problems were immediately referred for care, according to a protocol approved by the University of Minnesota Human Subjects Committee. Study procedures were administered by a physician (Minneapolis) and a nurse (Seattle).

STATISTICAL ANALYSIS

Response frequencies and means were computed for the suicide attempter and the nonattempter comparison groups. Independent samples X^2 and t tests were used to compare responses from the two groups. To limit the chance occurrence of significant findings, a .01 level of statistical significance was chosen for univariate analyses. Multiple logistic regression analysis was used to identify variables that were independently predictive of suicide attempts at a .05 level of significance.

RESULTS

Description of Suicide Attempts

Thirty percent of subjects (41/137) reported at least one suicide attempt, and almost half of the attempters (18/41) reported more than one attempt. A total of 68 suicide attempts were described and rated by Weisman and Worden's method. The mean age at the time of suicide attempts was 15.5 years. Ingestion of prescription and/or nonprescription drugs and self-laceration accounted for 80% of attempts. The remainder involved hangings, carbon monoxide poisonings, jumping, firearms, and automotive crashes. Twenty-one percent of the suicide attempts (14/68) resulted in medical or psychiatric hospitalization. Almost 3 out of 4 attempts (50/68) did not receive any medical attention. These included some attempts with high potential lethality, including two intentional car accidents, two carbon monoxide asphyxiations, and ingestions of large quantities of antidepressants, acetaminophen, aspirin, or intravenous heroin.

In 44% of cases, subjects attributed suicide attempts to "family problems," including conflict with family members and parents' marital discord, divorce, or alcoholism. One third of attempts were related to personal or interpersonal turmoil regarding homosexuality. Almost one third of subjects made their first suicide attempts in the same year that they identified themselves as bisexual or homosexual. Overall, three fourths of all first attempts temporally followed self-labeling. Other common precipitants were depression (30%), conflict with peers (22%), problems in a romantic relationship (19%), and dysphoria associated with personal substance abuse (15%). In one case, a suicide attempt followed notification of a partner's human immunodeficiency virus seropositivity.

Fifty-four percent of all suicide attempts (37/68) received risk scores in the "moderate to high" lethality range. The remaining attempts were of the "low risk" type. In one third of all cases (23/68), recovery was unassisted, and rescue scores could not be assigned by Weisman and Worden's criteria. These ranged from trivial injuries not needing treatment to severe insults with fortuitous recoveries. A rescue was initiated by the victim (24%) or by another person (76%) in the remaining 45 cases. Fifty-eight percent (26/45) of these cases received scores in the "moderate to least" rescuable range. In other words, the predicted likelihood of rescue was moderate to low, despite the actual occurrence of an intervention.

Table 2 depicts the distribution of risk and rescue scores for the 45 attempts for which both scores were available. Almost half of them (45%) were associated with moderate risk and moderate likelihood of rescue. Composite risk-rescue scores also were computed for these

TABLE 2. Number (and Percent Frequency Distribution) of Suicide Attempts (n=45), Classified by Likelihood of Risk and Rescue

Likelihood of Rescue	Risk of Morbidity/Mortality		
	Low	Moderate	High
Least	1 (2)	0	0
Moderate	5 (11)	20 (45)	1 (2)
Most	10 (22)	8 (18)	0

attempts. Thirty-six percent (18/45) received scores at or above Weisman and Worden's empirically derived mean (40) for adult attempters hospitalized in medical or psychiatric units.

Univariate Analyses

The following is a summary of the similarities and differences among the comparison groups. Further detail is provided in Table 3. There were no statistically significant differences ($P < .01$) between attempters and nonattempters with regard to age, educational level, race, religion, residence, or source of financial support. The majority of all participants (107/137, 78%) had received some type of professional mental health care. However, mean scores for current depression, hopelessness, and suicide intent (as measured by the respective instruments) were uniformly low for attempters and nonattempters. Also, no statistically significant ($P < .01$) differences were noted in the reported occurrence of depression, attempted or completed suicide, and psychiatric hospitalization among family members. Approximately one third of subjects in both groups were acquainted with a peer who had committed suicide.

Differences in gender role and sexual orientation development were prominent. Based on the Bem classification, attempters were more likely than nonattempters to be feminine or undifferentiated, and less likely to be masculine or androgynous ($P = .01$). Compared with nonattempters, attempters described themselves as bisexual or homosexual ($P = .002$) and shared this with other persons ($P = .005$) at younger ages. They also engaged in homosexual ($P = .0001$) and heterosexual activity ($P = .03$) to the point of orgasm at younger ages than their peers, although differences in the mean ages of first heterosexual activity were not statistically significant. As indicated by Table

TABLE 3. Psychosocial Characteristics (Mean and Percent Frequency Distribution [%F]) of Suicidal Attempters and Nonattempters

Variables	Attempters (n=41)	Nonattempters (n=96)	df	P value*
Sexual milestones: mean ages, y (SD)				
Earliest bi/homosexual attractions	9.27 (2.89)	10.66 (3.84)	130	.050
Bi/homosexual self-labeling	13.74 (3.22)	15.44 (2.61)	132	.002
First homosexual experience	14.38 (2.48)	16.13 (2.54)	129	.000
First heterosexual experience	14.61 (2.56)	16.10 (1.87)	57	.030
"Coming out" to others	15.62 (2.92)	16.95 (2.22)	128	.005
Psychosocial stressors, %F				
Parents' marital status				
Unmarried	7	6		
Divorced	61	42	3	.08
Married	27	50		
Mother knows son's sexuality	87	81	1	.44
Supportive maternal response	32	38	4	.62
Father knows son's sexuality	65	56	1	.45
Supportive paternal response	23	15	4	.58
Friendship loss	42	28	1	.18
Peer suicide	39	27	1	.24
Discrimination	61	46	1	.15
Violence	39	38	1	1.00
Sexual abuse	61	29	1	.0008
Psychosocial problems, %F				
Running away	49	36	1	.25
Arrest	51	28	1	.01
Prostitution	29	17	1	.20
Ethanol ever use	78	83	1	.62
Illicit drug use	85	63	1	.01
Personal mental health, %F				
Any mental health services	88	74	1	.12
Chemical dependency treatment	22	6	1	.01
No current suicide intent (item from Scale for Suicide Ideation)	68	84	1	.06
No suicide plan (item from Scale for Suicide Ideation)	93	98	1	.32
Family mental health,** %F				
Depression	43	40	1	.92
Attempted/complete suicide	38	22	1	.12
Psychiatric hospitalization	44	45	1	.12
Psychometric indices: mean scores (SD)				
Beck Depression Inventory	10.78 (8.60)	7.68 (7.20)	135	.03
Scale for Suicide Ideation	6.90 (6.40)	4.61 (4.50)	135	.04
Hopelessness Scale	4.37 (0.50)	2.90 (0.40)	135	.10
Attitudes toward homosexuality	56.24 (14.5)	56.35 (0.19)	133	.97
Bem-masculinity raw score	4.75 (0.66)	5.04 (0.79)	135	.04
Bem-femininity raw score	5.08 (0.66)	4.91 (0.61)	135	.15
Bem classification, %F				
Masculine	7.3	26.0		
Feminine	36.6	17.7		
Androgynous	26.8	32.3	3	.01
Undifferentiated	29.3	24.0		

*P values correspond to X^2 tests for nominal variables and t tests for continuous variables.

**Includes first- to third-degree relatives.

3, bisexual or homosexual self-identification generally preceded first sexual experiences with either gender.

Suicide attempters were more likely than nonattempters (P = .0008) to report sexual abuse, broadly defined as being forced, pressured or tricked to have sex. Detailed descriptions of incidents were not obtained. Twenty-nine percent of attempters and 17% of nonattempters accepted money for sex on at least one occasion. Both groups reported similar personal attitudes toward homosexuality, reactions from parents and friends, and experiences with discrimination and violence.

Compared with peers, a larger proportion of attempters reported illicit drug use (85% vs. 63%, P = .01) and arrest for criminal activities (51% vs. 28%, P = .01). Twenty-two percent of attempters (vs. 6% of nonattempters, P = .01) had undergone chemical dependency treatment. Theft (40%) and possession of illicit substances (20%) accounted for the majority of reported arrests. The remaining violations included assault, vandalism, disorderly conduct, disturbing the peace, trespassing, prostitution, and other sex offenses.

Multivariate Analyses

The univariate analyses revealed a total of nine variables that were associated with suicide attempts at the .01 level of statistical significance. Multiple logistic regression analysis was undertaken to identify which were predictive of attempts, when controlling for the other variables. Of the nine variables, five were entered into the analysis based on their conceptual inclusivity and completeness of ascertainment in this study. From the four items related to sexual milestones, age at the time of bisexual or homosexual self-labeling was selected. From the two items regarding substance abuse, ever use of illegal drugs was chosen. Finally, feminine gender role, criminal apprehension, and sexual abuse were included. All five variables were obtained in 96% (132/137) of cases.

Based on the multiple logistic regression analysis, ever use of illicit drugs, feminine gender role, and age at the time of bisexual or homosexual self-labeling were independently associated with suicide attempts at the .05 level of statistical significance (Table 4). Feminine gender roles and illicit drug use each were associated with greater than a threefold risk of attempted suicide. According to the model, the likelihood of an attempt diminished with advancing age at the time of bisexual or homosexual self-labeling. With each year's delay in self-identification, the odds of a suicide attempt declined by more than 80%.

DISCUSSION

Approximately one third of gay and bisexual youth in this study reported at least one intentional self-destructive act, and almost half of them repeatedly attempted suicide. The gravity of some attempts is reflected in the rate of subsequent hospitalization (21%), the lethality of methods (54%, moderate to high risk), and the victims' inaccessibility to rescue (62%, moderate to least rescuable). The findings support psychiatrists' concerns about the severity of suicide attempts among homosexual youth.[9]

In this sample, bisexuality or homosexuality per se was not associated with self-destructive acts. Most of the subjects did not attempt or plan suicide. However, from the perspective of many attempters, sexual concerns were circumstantially or temporally related to self-harm. One third of all suicide attempts were attributed to personal or interpersonal turmoil about homosexuality. One third of first attempts occurred in the same year that subjects identified their bisexuality or homosexuality, and most other attempts happened soon thereafter. The apparent connection between sexual milestones and attempts may be a clue to the appropriate timing of suicide prevention efforts.

Based on the univariate analyses, suicide attempts were not explained by experiences with discrimination, violence, loss of friendship, or current personal attitudes toward homosexuality. Unlike other reports,[18] this study did not find a significant association between attempts and running away from home. However, gender nonconformity and precocious psychosexual development were predictive of self-harm. Compared with peers, suicide attempters recognized homosexual attractions and told other persons at younger ages. First sexual experiences with males and females also occurred at younger ages than peers'. For each year's delay in bisexual or homosexual self-labeling, the odds of a suicide attempt diminished by 80%. These findings support a previously observed, inverse relationship between psychosocial problems and the age of acquiring a homosexual iden-

TABLE 4. Summary Table: Regression Analysis of Suicide Attempts

Variable	Odds Ratio	95% Confidence Interval	Regression Coefficient	SE	P Value
Constant	...	...	0.24	1.24	...
Label age	0.82	0.69–0.96	–0.21	0.08	0.01
Drug use	3.63	1.07–12.24	1.29	0.61	0.03
Feminine	3.03	1.10–8.31	1.11	0.50	0.03
Sex abuse	2.23	0.90–5.53	0.81	0.45	0.08
Arrest	1.87	0.74–4.67	0.62	0.46	0.06

tity.[8] Compared with older persons, early and middle adolescents may be generally less able to cope with the isolation and stigma of a homosexual identity.

A feminine or undifferentiated gender role may accentuate a gay adolescent's sense of "differentness" and further exacerbate problems.[19] Severely gender-atypical male children have been observed to experience a "pervasive psychological disturbance"[20] and an "abnormal amount of depression and social conflict resulting from peer rejection, isolation, and ridicule of their feminine behavior."[21] In general, masculine and androgynous boys and girls alike have better self-esteem[22] and lower rates of substance use and psychological distress[23] than feminine or undifferentiated youth. Among male and female college students, masculinity and androgyny are associated with positive adjustment to stress[24] and minimal fearfulness.[25]

The univariate analyses also revealed an association between sexual abuse and suicide attempts. However, when controlling for other variables in the multiple regression analysis, sexual abuse was not a statistically significant predictor. The contribution of sexual abuse to suicide risk may have been subsumed by other variables such as drug use or gender atypicality. For example, gender-atypical boys may be vulnerable to sexual assault, as well as suicide. Alternatively, abused boys may develop substance abuse problems that heighten suicide risk. Also noteworthy, sexual abuse did not appear to have a major impact on sexual identity, because bisexual or homosexual identification usually preceded sexual experiences.

The attempters in this study resembled actual suicide victims in regard to high levels of family dysfunction,[26–29] personal substance abuse,[28–34] and other antisocial behaviors.[27,32,35] Family problems were the most frequently cited reasons for attempts. Eighty-five percent of attempters reported illicit drug use, and 22% had undergone chemical dependency treatment. More than half (21/41) of the attempters had been arrested for misconduct. Like other boys who eventually complete suicide,[26,35,36] many subjects made multiple unsuccessful attempts. In general, many of the psychosocial problems associated with gay suicide attempts (e.g., family discord, substance abuse, and conflict with the law) are familiar correlates of completed youth suicide. Such problems often complicate "coming out" at an early age[8] and may further contribute to the high rate of suicide in this group.

   In contrast to some of the psychological autopsies of young victims,[26,31,35] this study found low levels of active depression, hopelessness, and suicidal intent among attempters. Moreover, the attempters and nonattempters had similar family histories of depression, suicide, and psychiatric hospitalization. Although chronic or heritable forms of depression did not account for suicide attempts in this group, the results must be interpreted cautiously. Acute depression and hopelessness at the time of the attempt may have since lifted with treatment or the passage of time, and subjects may not have been well informed of family mental histories.

   The circumstances, prevalence, and severity of suicide attempts in this cohort may not reflect the general population of homosexually oriented boys and girls. Because of the social stigma of homosexuality, a probability sampling of homosexual youth was unfeasible. However, an effort was made to enhance the generalizability of the findings by recruiting subjects from diverse settings and geographical areas. Gay-identified adolescents are a subset of all youth who will eventually disclose a homosexual orientation.[37] As our own findings suggest, the experiences of openly gay and bisexual youth may be quite different from those of other boys who are confused, hiding, or delayed in identifying sexual feelings. Likewise, the risks for suicide among lesbian girls may be quite different from those among boys because of the gender, gender role, sexual identity development, and cultural differences.

   Acknowledging these limitations, the unusual prevalence of serious suicide attempts remains a consistent and disturbing finding in the existing reports of young homosexual males. The rate of completed suicide among homosexual attempters is unknown, as is the relative contribution of homosexual adolescents to total youth suicides. These issues merit further investigation to illuminate the epidemiology of adolescent suicide, the direction of suicide prevention programs, and the care of individual clients. We hope that this study's findings will lead to other investigations of sexuality and suicide among representative samples of youth in schools or other community settings. Ultimately, the study of suicide among gay and bisexual youth may shed new light on the unifying characteristics of adolescent victims, unraveling the common threads of risk which transcend the issue of sexual orientation.

ACKNOWLEDGMENTS

This work was supported, in part, by grants from the Bureau of Maternal and Child Health and Resource Development (MCJ-000985) and the Grant-in-Aid Program of the Graduate School, University of Minnesota.

Statistical consultation was provided by Kinley Larntz, Ph.D., Professor of Statistics. Special thanks to Robert Blum, M.D., Kevin Cwayna, M.D., Barry Garfinkel, M.D., Mary Story, Ph.D., Kenneth Winters, Ph.D., and John Yoakam, M.Div., for their consultation and to Dean McWilliams, Joy Love, M.Div., and W.S. Foster for their technical assistance.

REFERENCES

1. National Center for Health Statistics (1986). *Vital statistics of the United States: Vol. 2. Mortality*, Part A. Hyattsville, MD: Author.

2. Hoberman, H.M. (1989). Completed suicide in children and adolescents: A review. *Residential Treatment for Children and Youth, 7*, 61–88.

3. Remafedi, G. (1988). Adolescent homosexuality: A challenge to contemporary society. *Journal of the American Medical Association, 258*, 222–225.

4. Jay, K., and Young, A. (Eds.) (1979). *The gay report: Lesbians and gay men speak out about their sexual experiences and lifestyles*. New York: Simon & Schuster.

5. Bell, A., and Weinberg, M. (1978). *Homosexualities: A study of diversity among men and women*. New York: Simon & Schuster.

6. Saghir, M.T., and Robins, E. (1973). *Male and female homosexuality: A comprehensive investigation*. Baltimore, MD: Williams & Wilkins.

7. Roesler, T., and Deisher, R.W. (1972). Youthful male homosexuality. *Journal of the American Medical Association, 219*, 1018–1023.

8. Remafedi, G. (1987). Adolescent homosexuality: Psychosocial and medical implications. *Pediatrics, 79*, 331–337.

9. Kourany, R.F. (1987). Suicide among homosexual adolescents. *Journal of Homosexuality, 13*(4), 111–117.

10. U.S. Department of Health and Human Services (1989). *Report of the Secretary's Task Force on Youth Suicide: Vol. 3. Prevention and interventions in youth suicide.* Rockville, MD: Author.

11. Remafedi, G. (1987). Male homosexuality: The adolescent's perspective. *Pediatrics, 79*, 326–330.

12. Weisman, A.D., and Worden, J.W. (1972). Risk-rescue rating in suicide assessment. *Archives of General Psychiatry, 26*, 553–560.

13. Beck, A.T., Kovacs, M., and Weissman, A. (1979). Assessment of suicidal intention: The scale for suicide ideation. *Journal of Consulting and Clinical Psychology, 47*, 343–352

14. Bem, S. (1974). The measurement of psychological androgyny. *Journal of Consulting and Clinical Psychology, 42*, 155–162.

15. Beck, A.T., Ward, C.H., Mendelson, M., et al. (1961). An inventory for measuring depression. *Archives of General Psychiatry, 4*, 561–571.

16. Beck, A.T., Weissman, A., Lester, D., et al. (1974). The measurement of pessimism: The Hopelessness Scale. *Journal of Consulting and Clinical Psychology, 42*, 861–865.

17. Price, J.H. (1982). High school students' attitudes toward homosexuality. *Journal of School Health, 52*, 469–474.

18. Rotheram, M.J. (1987). Evaluation of imminent danger for suicide among youth. *American Journal of Orthopsychiatry, 57*, 102–110.

19. Martin, A.D. (1982). Learning to hide: The socialization of the gay adolescent. *Adolescent Psychiatry, 10*, 52–65.

20. Coates, S., and Person, E.S. (1985). Extreme boyhood femininity: Isolated behavior or pervasive disorder. *Journal of the American Academy of Child Psychiatry, 24*, 702–709.

21. Rosen, A.C., Rekers, G.A., and Friar, L.R. (1977). Theoretical and diagnostic issues in child gender disturbances. *Journal of Sex Research, 13*, 89–103.

22. Lamke, L.K. (1982). The impact of sex-role orientation of self-esteem in early adolescence. *Child Development, 53*, 1530–1535.

23. Horwitz, A.V., and White, H.R. (1987). Gender role orientations and styles of pathology among adolescents. *Journal of Health and Social Behavior, 28*, 158–170.

24. Roos, P.E., and Cohen, L.H. (1987). Sex roles and social support as moderators of life stress adjustment. *Journal of Personality and Social Psychology, 3*, 576–585.

25. Dillon, K.M., Wolf, E., and Katz, H. (1985). Sex roles, gender, and fear. *Journal of Psychology, 119*, 355–359.

26. Thompson, T.R. (1987). Childhood and adolescent suicide in Manitoba: A demographic study. *Canadian Journal of Psychiatry, 32*, 264–269.

27. Shaffer, D. (1974). Suicide in childhood and early adolescence. *Journal of Child Psychology and Psychiatry, 15*, 275–291.

28. Hoberman, H.M., and Garfinkel, B.D. (1988). Completed suicide in children and adolescents. *Journal of the American Academy of Child and Adolescent Psychiatry, 27,* 689–695.

29. Peck, M. (1984). Suicide in late adolescence and young adulthood. In C.L. Hatton and S.M. Velenti (Eds.), *Suicide: Assessment and intervention* (pp. 220–230). Norwalk, CT: Appleton-Century-Crofts.

30. Brent, D.A., Perper, J.A., Goldstein, C.E., et al. (1988). Risk factors for adolescent suicide. *Archives of General Psychiatry, 45,* 581–588.

31. Poteet, D.J. (1987). Adolescent suicide: A review of 87 cases of completed suicide in Shelby County, Tennessee. *American Journal of Forensic Medicine and Pathology, 8,* 12–17.

32. Shaffer, D. (1988). The epidemiology of teen suicide: An examination of risk factors. *Journal of Clinical Psychiatry, 49,* 36–41.

33. Slap, G.B., Vorters, D.F., Chaudhuri, S., and Centor, R.M. (1989). Risk factors for attempted suicide during adolescence. *Pediatrics, 84,* 762–772.

34. Rich, C.L., Fowler, R.C., Young, D., and Blenkush, M. (1986). San Diego suicide study: Comparison of gay to straight males. *Suicide and Life-Threatening Behavior, 16*(4), 448–457.

35. Shaffi, N., Carrigan, S., Whittingill, J.R., and Derric, A. (1985). Psychology autopsy of completed suicide in children and adolescents. *American Journal of Psychiatry, 142,* 1061–1064.

36. Cosand, B.J., Bourque, M.L., and Krauss J.F. (1982). Suicide among adolescents in Sacramento County, California, 1950–1979. *Adolescence, 17,* 917–930.

37. Remafedi, G. (1990). Adolescent homosexuality. *Medical Clinics of North America, 74,* 1169–1179.

San Diego Suicide Study: Comparison of Gay to Straight Males

CHARLES L. RICH, M.D.
University of California at San Diego, School of Medicine,
San Diego Veterans Administration Medical Center

RICHARD C. FOWLER, M.D.
University of California at San Diego, School of Medicine

DEBORAH YOUNG, M.D.
University of California at San Diego, School of Medicine

and MARY BLENKUSH, M.D.
University of California at San Diego, School of Medicine

From *Suicide and Life-Threatening Behavior, 16*(4)
(Winter 1986), 448–457.

ABSTRACT: *Previous large studies of completed suicides have not considered sexual orientation in their data analyses. In this study, data from the known homosexual subpopulation (13 males, aged 21–42) in a series of 283 suicides were examined. They were compared with all other aged male suicides 21–42 (n = 106). Both groups showed considerable substance abuse plus a variety of other psychiatric diagnoses. Both also had a high frequency of relationship difficulties near the time of death. Gays who committed suicide did not have a history of more police trouble and were no more likely to be*

living alone than the comparison group. They did not have more prior
suicide attempts or previous psychiatric treatment. We conclude that,
among the factors examined here, there appears to be little difference
between gay and heterosexual male suicides.

In previous studies of large series of suicides, sexual orientation has not been one of the demographic factors identified (Barraclough, Bunch, Nelson, & Sainsbury, 1974; Beskow, 1979; Chynoweth, Tonge, & Armstrong, 1980; Dorpat & Ripley, 1960; Morrison, 1982; Ovenstone, 1973; Pokorny, 1983; Robins, 1981; Roy, 1982; Seager & Flood, 1965). Studies of homosexual samples, however, have shown rates of certain suicide risk factors, including substance abuse, psychiatric treatment, and suicide attempts, to be higher than in heterosexual comparison groups (Fifield, 1975; Saghir & Robins, 1973). Because of the apparent increased prevalence of these risk factors, one might suspect that the suicide rate would be higher in the gay population. This is impossible to assess, though, as the size of the gay population is not known. Nonetheless, various subpopulations such as gays should be examined to see whether individual factors or patterns might set them apart in terms of assessing suicide risk in the clinical setting.

This study utilized extensive clinical information gathered on 283 suicides. We looked for differences between gay and other suicides that might aid clinicians in assessing the suicide risk of potentially suicidal gays.

METHODS

With the assistance of the San Diego County Coroner's Office, 283 cases of suicide (202 males, 81 females) were identified from November 1981 through June 1983. The first 204 cases were collected consecutively. The remainder were consecutive cases under age 30. Thus the sample consisted of 133 consecutive cases under age 30 and 150 consecutive cases age 30 and over.

Names of potential informants were obtained from the reports filed by the deputy coroners. These potential informants consisted of family members, spouses, acquaintances, employers, other witnesses, physicians, and other professionals. Trained interviewers obtained extensive information on psychiatric symptoms, life events, and medical and family history. They used a structured interview containing over 300 items designed to obtain information about all DSM-III (American Psychiatric Association, 1980) diagnoses, as well as other clinical issues considered relevant to the subject of suicide. Information was also sought from hospital, school, police, and other records.

Following completion of the clinical investigation, each case was independently reviewed by two of us. Each of these two made diagnoses based on DSM-III criteria for the first three axes. This required the judgment of the two investigators when the information was incomplete. For example, substance use typically lasted more than a month and caused definite psychosocial problems, but information regarding patterns of pathological use may not have been clear. Over 90% of the diagnostic assessments were done by C.L.R. and R.C.F., the remainder being done by D.Y. After the independent assessments, each case was reviewed by the two investigators together to attempt to reconcile disagreements. When this could not be done, the third investigator was asked to render an independent judgment. This was only necessary in one case.

Homosexuals were identified as those who by history had predominantly or exclusively homosexual relationships and considered themselves homosexual. Equivocal cases (e.g., a young male with a frequency of homosexual activity, usually for money, who considered himself heterosexual and had a history of sexual relationships with women) were included in the heterosexual group because of expressed preference for heterosexual activity. Since all of the homosexuals so defined ($n = 13$) were males between the ages of 21 and 42, the remainder of the males in that age range ($n = 106$) were used for a comparison group.

All the variables selected for comparisons are reported here. Their selection was based on their hypothetical relevance to this analysis. Data were analyzed using chi-squares with Yates's correction. A probability of less than .05 was considered significant.

RESULTS

A mean of 2.6 (range 1–6) interviews were obtained for the 13 gay cases, compared to a mean of 1.6 (range 0–5) for the 106 straights.

Medical records were available for 7 of the 13 gays and 44 of the 106 straights.

Table 1 shows some of the important clinical characteristics of each case. Only one case (case no. 13) had ever been married; he was separated at the time of death. Two lived alone, four with parents, and seven with one or more roommates. Known suicide attempts were as common in the gay group as in the comparison group (8 of 12 vs. 34 of 91). There was also no difference between the groups in how many were known to have ever had psychiatric treatment (10 of 13 vs. 46 of 89). Hanging was used as a method by the gay group significantly more often (6 of 13 vs. 12 of 106; $X^2 = 8.40, p = .004$). There were no significant differences in childhood or adult legal problems for the cases in which this information was known (Table 2). For all of these comparisons, there were no significant differences in the number of cases with missing information. The chi-squares for these data were recalculated using the most extreme possibilities to compensate for missing data. For example, the values for previous attempts were calculated for 9 of 13 versus 34 of 106 and 8 of 13 versus 49 of 106. In the cases of previous attempts and prior treatment, these calculations suggested that the gays might have been overrepresented. In relation to the legal problems, the only effect this had was to show the possibility that the straight subjects might have had more jailings and/or convictions.

Table 3 lists the psychiatric diagnoses and stressors for each gay case. Of the 13 gay suicides, 12 had one or more DSM-III substance abuse diagnoses. All but two had a diagnosis other than substance abuse. Only schizophrenia occurred more frequently in the gays than the comparison group (Table 4). There were no significant differences in general categories of stressors between the gays and the other males.

DISCUSSION

Before discussing the findings in detail, we should describe our decision-making process regarding reliability and validity of the data base. We did not weigh the validity of sources of information *a priori*. We generally found that some sources were poorly informed in specific areas. Parents and physicians, for example, typically knew little about drug abuse that was common knowledge to friends. Likewise,

TABLE 1. Clinical Characteristics of Gay Suicides

Case no.	Age	Living with	Previous attempts	Psychiatric treatment ever	Method
1	21	Male friend	Yes	No	Gun
2	21	Parents	No	Yes	Jumping
3	23	Male friend	?	Yes	Hanging
4	23	Friend	No	Yes	Burning
5	24	Live-in aide	Yes	Yes	Overdose
6	26	Parents	Yes	Yes	Hanging
7	27	Friends	Yes	Yes	Jumping
8	28	Mother	Yes	Yes	Overdose
9	28	Father	No	Yes	Hanging
10	33	Friend	No	No	Hanging
11	34	Alone	Yes	Yes	Hanging
12	40	Alone	Yes	Yes	Overdose
13	42	Alone	Yes	No	Hanging

each informant might have noticed one or two depressive symptoms that were different from the ones someone else observed. Even siblings occasionally disagreed about how many siblings were in the family and whether the parents were alive. While this variability among informants may be unsettling to some, we believe it is an inherent problem of this type of research. For better or worse, we attempted to determine what seemed to be the correct answer for each question based on all the available information. This is a reality that clinicians face daily.

The findings in this study suggest that there may be few if any differences between young gay and straight males who commit suicide. Before reaching such a conclusion or generalizing it to all homosexual persons, however, several limitations in the present sample must be addressed.

TABLE 2. Legal Problems

Problem	Gay (n =13)	Other (n =106)
Legal problems as child	5/11	29/80
Ever arrested	6/11	62/91
Ever jailed	0/9	22/84
Ever convicted	2/11	38/84

Note: Denominator indicates number of cases for which this information was available.

TABLE 3. Diagnoses and Stressors in Gay Suicides

Case no.	Psychiatric diagnoses		Stressors
	Drug/alcohol abuse	Other diagnoses	
1	Both	Atypical depression	Relationship terminated; financial straits
2	Both	—	Relationship terminated; trial pending
3	Both	Adjustment disorder with depression	Relationship terminated; unemployed; change of residence
4	Drug	Atypical psychosis	Employer criticism; financial straits
5	Both	—	Financial straits
6	Drug	Atypical depression	Relationship terminated; parental conflict; job problems; financial straits; change of residence
7	Both	Schizophrenia	Relationship terminated; parental conflict; unemployed
8	Drug	Atypical depression	Death of mother
9	Both	Schizophrenia	None
10	Drug	Schizoaffective	Relationship terminated
11	Both	Atypical psychosis	Change of residence
12	Alcohol	Schizophrenia	Relationship terminated
13	—	Dysthymic	Death of son

First, since suicide is a relatively infrequent cause of death overall, it becomes even more difficult to generate a large sample of suicides from a minority group to study. A sample size of 13 is hardly adequate to justify highly sophisticated statistical analysis or any other major conclusions. It is, however, the largest sample reported to date that has been studied so extensively.

The second problem is that the true rate of homosexuality (regardless of the functional definition) in the population is unknown. Before one can really ask the question about the suicide rate in a subpopulation, one obviously has to know the size of the group. Even though we had no women or men over age 42, the rate we found of about 10% in the males aged 21–42 reflects a generally accepted population rate. This adds support to the conclusion that gays do not have a higher suicide rate than straights. We did not (and do not) know, however, what the rate of male homosexuality is in the San Diego area. It seems unlikely that we will be sure about that population rate for some time to come. We also had no way of knowing what the rate of covert

TABLE 4. Diagnoses and Stressors in Gay versus Comparison Suicides

Diagnosis/stressor	Gay (n =13)	Other (n =106)	X^2
Diagnoses			
Drug abuse only	4	25	0.052
Alcohol abuse only	1	6	0.109
Drug + alcohol abuse	7	48	0.084
Neither	1	27	1.166
Schizophrenia	3	3	6.137*
Schizoaffective	1	5	0.044
Atypical psychosis	2	12	0.001
Total psychotic	6	20	3.578
Dysthymic disorder	1	2	0.104
Adjustment disorder	1	9	0.186
Atypical depression	3	30	0.005
Total depressive	5	41	0.082
Stressors			
Relationship terminated	7	38	0.921
Financial problems	5	24	0.831
Legal problems	1	11	0.034
Job problems	4	40	0.035
Change of residence	3	11	0.784

*p = .013

homosexuality might have been among the comparison subjects. Consequently, we decided to use all the males aged 21–42 who were not known to be homosexual (as we defined it), so as to minimize the effect of inadvertent inclusion of gays in the comparison group.

Third, the fact that our gay group consisted entirely of males under age 43 suggests a limitation in case identification. It is hard to imagine that there were no gay males over age 42, since there were 83 males in that age range. On the basis of the 10% population estimate mentioned above, we might have expected to find 8 or so gays in that group. Nonetheless, if it were true, it might pose an interesting clinical question — namely, does homosexuality protect older men from suicide? The apparent absence of lesbians in the study sample of 81 women is perhaps no less surprising. Again, the actual population rate of lesbianism is unknown, but 10% seems to be generally accepted. If our detection rate was accurate, we possibly have evidence supporting the hypothesis that, like older gays, lesbians commit suicide at a lower rate than straight women. Other possible explanations must be considered, of course. For example, it might be that women and older men are more motivated to conceal their homosexuality. It is also possible that the fewer, more stable relationships lesbians generally engage in might be a factor. The reason for our case distribution is another interesting topic for further study.

The fourth problem is in dealing with geographic variation in population characteristics. Not only do suicide rates vary from region to region, but so probably does the rate of homosexuality (or any population characteristic one cares to measure). In addition, the "character" of a subpopulation may vary on a geographic basis. It would be improper, then, to assume that young male homosexuals who commit suicide in San Diego are like those in other areas. Future studies must look at this question when comparing their results to ours.

Even with all these caveats, we feel it is important to look systematically at this subpopulation. We do feel that it is at least sufficient to provide some direction for future studies to follow.

Social isolation and oppression have been hypothesized to be higher in gays, with resultant increases in substance abuse, psychiatric problems, and suicide (Saunders & Valente, 1984). However, few gays in our sample lived alone, and they had no apparent increases in arrests or other legal problems. While there may be more sensitive indicators of the quality of oppression and isolation, such information is very hard to infer from postmortem informant interviews.

Establishing sexual identity is unquestionably a tumultuous time for homosexuals. This could also be hypothesized as a cause of the focus of gay suicides in younger years. We found, however, that the stressors associated with our gay suicides were really no different from those associated with the comparison subjects. Again, we cannot determine whether the quality of the stressors is the same for both groups. For example, is it more disturbing for a heterosexual couple to break up in our society than a homosexual one? Gay relationships in this age group may be shorter lived than heterosexual marriages, but it is impossible really to measure the energy invested in either type of commitment. On the surface, at least, it appears that the stressors faced by gays who commit suicide are categorically similar to those of their straight counterparts.

All of the gay suicides had a psychiatric diagnosis, but this is not out of line with the fact that over 90% of the total 283 cases had such diagnoses (Rich, Young, & Fowler, 1986). This is also consistent with the studies cited in the first part of this paper. The occurrence of multiple diagnoses, particularly in those with drug and/or alcohol abuse, was also not uncommon in our total sample.

Evidence suggests that gay men from selected populations have a higher incidence of drug abuse and alcoholism than age-matched single heterosexual males (Fifield, 1975; Lohrenz, Connelly, Coyne, & Spare, 1978; Saghir & Robins, 1973). It is not clear from this or other studies whether the homosexual life style is causally or coincidentally related to the substance abuse. Interestingly, our data suggests that drugs and alcohol play a major role in as many suicides among straights as gays in this age group. To assess whether homosexuality itself is a risk factor would require following a large group of gays (including controls matched for drug and/or alcohol abuse) for a considerable time. Regardless of which comes first, it is obviously important to pay heed to the presence of substance abuse when clinically assessing anyone's suicide risk.

The frequency of schizophrenia as a diagnosis among the gays in our sample seems high. We believe, however, that it would be inappropriate to make too much of that, because of the small sample size. It is important to realize that all three of the schizophrenics also had substance abuse diagnoses. We will be looking at the problem of multiple diagnoses as risk factors for suicide in subsequent reports.

Previous psychiatric treatment was found by Saghir and Robins (1973) to be more frequent among gays than among single heterosexuals. Our gay group also had more previous treatment (77% vs. 52%), but the difference was not significant. We found that young drug abusers (under age 30) without other diagnoses actually had received significantly less previous treatment than had suicides with other diagnoses (Fowler, Rich, & Young, 1990). This may account for the lack of difference in this study, but the fact remains that a majority of both gays and straights had had previous treatment. Again, while this does not set gays apart, it is a consideration in assessing their suicide risk clinically.

No more gays than straights in our sample were known to have made suicide attempts. In their study of gay males, Saghir and Robins (1973) found that 7% of the gays and none of the controls had made attempts, but the difference was not significant. Likewise, we did not find a greater previous attempt rate in the young drug abusers who committed suicide. (Fowler et al., 1990). While previous attempts are also generally accepted as risk factors for suicide, their false-positive rate is so high as to severely limit their clinical usefulness. This is probably also true for the gay subpopulation. It is interesting to note, however, that only a slightly larger sample size of gays (18 cases) with the same ratio of attempts (67%) would have produced a significant difference from the comparisons.

Finally, the frequency of hanging among the gays as a suicide method was unexpected. None of the six gay hangings was associated with sexual activity. The one case of possible sexual asphyxia in the total study sample was not known to be gay. While this finding still may lend itself to interesting psychodynamic speculation, it has very little clinical relevance. Removing guns from a suicidal person's presence is easy, compared to removing means of hanging. If this finding proves consistent, however, it would point to the need for special precautions against hanging when suicidal gays are admitted to inpatient services.

In conclusion, we feel that our data demonstrate very little difference between our gay suicides and their age-matched straight counterparts. Clearly, studies of larger samples will be needed to check these findings. Unless differences are demonstrated in the future, however, clinicians should pay attention to the same sorts of warning signals in their gay patients as they would in heterosexuals.

NOTE

This work was supported by the Veterans Administration. An earlier version of this paper was presented at the meeting of the American Academy of Clinical Psychiatrists, San Francisco, October 1985. We wish to thank the San Diego County Coroner, David Stark, and his staff for their generous assistance with this project. We especially thank Richard Shaw, the Coroner's Chief Chemist, and his staff for their dedication to organizing and performing the toxicological examinations. Finally, we gratefully acknowledge the following persons for their sensitive, thoughtful, and devoted attention to the data gathering, collation, and analysis: Sunny Ballishi, Nancy Black, Jackie Cape, Karen Elhai, Steven Ferguson, Linda Fogarty, Alan Lai, Mal Lambert, Debra Lobatz, Gene Morris, John Motay, Mitchell Motooka, Richard Okamura, Christian Paul, Sharon K.S. Rosenfeld, and Donald Volk.

REFERENCES

American Psychiatric Association (1980). *Diagnostic and statistical manual of mental disorders* (3rd ed.). Washington, DC: Author.

Barraclough, B., Bunch, J., Nelson, B., and Sainsbury, P. (1974). A hundred cases of suicide: Clinical aspects. *British Journal of Psychiatry, 125*, 355–373.

Beskow, J. (1979). Suicide and mental disorder in Swedish men. *Acta Psychiatrica Scandinavica* (Suppl. 277).

Chynoweth, R., Tonge, J.I., and Armstrong, J. (1980). Suicide in Brisbane: A retrospective psychosocial study. *Australia and New Zealand Journal of Psychiatry, 14*, 37–45.

Dorpat, T., and Ripley, H. (1960). A study of suicide in the Seattle area. *Comprehensive Psychiatry, 1*, 349–359.

Fifield, L. (1975). *On my way to nowhere: Alienated, isolated, drunk.* Los Angeles: The Gay Community Services Center.

Fowler, R.C., Rich, C.L., and Young, D. (1990, Winter). The San Diego suicide study: Drug abuse in young cases. *Archives of General Psychiatry, 25*(100), 855–865.

Lohrenz, L.J., Connelly, J.K.C., Coyne, L., and Spare, K.E. (1978). Alcohol problems in several Midwestern homosexual communities. *Journal of Studies on Alcohol, 11*, 1959–1963.

Morrison, J.R. (1982). Suicide in a psychiatric practice population. *Journal of Clinical Psychiatry, 43*, 348–352.

Ovenstone, I.M.K. (1973). Spectrum of suicidal behaviors in Edinburgh. *British Journal of Preventative and Social Medicine, 27*, 27–35.

Pokorny, A.D. (1983). Prediction of suicide in psychiatric patients: Report of a prospective study. *Archives of General Psychiatry, 40*, 249–257.

Rich, C.L., Young, D., and Fowler, R.C. (1986). San Diego suicide study: Young versus old cases. *Archives of General Psychiatry, 43*, 577–582.

Robins, E. (1981). *The final months: A study of the lives of 134 persons who committed suicide.* New York: Oxford University Press.

Roy, A. (1982). Risk factors for suicide in psychiatric patients. *Archives of General Psychiatry, 39*, 1089–1095.

Saghir, M., and Robins, E. (1973). *Male and female homosexuality: A comprehensive investigation.* Baltimore, MD: Williams & Wilkins.

Saunders, J., and Valente, S. (1984). *Suicide and homosexuality: Exploration of a potential relationship.* Paper presented at the annual meeting of the American Association of Suicidology, Anchorage, Alaska.

Seager, C.P., and Flood, R.A. (1965). Suicide in Bristol. *British Journal of Psychiatry, 111*, 919–932.

Making Schools Safe for Gay and Lesbian Youth

Breaking the silence in schools and in families

THE MASSACHUSETTS GOVERNOR'S COMMISSION ON GAY AND LESBIAN YOUTH

Education Report, February 25, 1993;
Publication No. 17296-60-500-2/93-C.R.

EXECUTIVE SUMMARY

*Formation and mandate of nation's
first gay and lesbian youth commission*

Governor William F. Weld [of Massachusetts] signed an executive order on February 10th, 1992, creating the nation's first Governor's Commission on Gay and Lesbian Youth. Governor Weld and Lieutenant Governor Paul Cellucci formed the Commission in response to the epidemic of suicide by young gays and lesbians as revealed in a 1989 Federal report on youth suicide.

The Governor's Commission on Gay and Lesbian Youth is the first commission of its kind in the United States.

Prevention of gay and lesbian youth suicide, violence prevention, as well as prevention of problems faced by young gays and lesbians in school and in the family are central to the Commission's mandate. The Commission is empowered to make recommendations to the

Governor, to state agencies, and to private agencies about the creation of programs and policies which will help gay and lesbian youth in Massachusetts. Abolishing prejudice and discrimination against gay and lesbian youth is a stated goal of the Commission as expressed by Governor Weld in the preamble to the executive order.

The Commission exists on an ongoing basis as an all-volunteer advocacy group, serving under the auspices of the Weld/Cellucci administration. The Commission is charged with making an annual report to Governor Weld.

Identifying problems faced by gay and lesbian youth in school

This first report of the Commission is its Education Report, entitled "Making Schools Safe for Gay and Lesbian Youth." In this report, the Commission addresses the problems faced by gay and lesbian adolescents in schools. To gather information for its report, the Commission held a series of five public hearings across Massachusetts in the autumn of 1992. The hearings were held in Amherst on November 13, Worcester on November 16, the Massachusetts State House on November 17 and November 18, and finally in Springfield on December 1. The hearings were open to the general public and to the media.

The Education Report of the Governor's Commission on Gay and Lesbian Youth focuses on the testimony delivered by gay and lesbian teenagers as compelling evidence for the need for change in Massachusetts schools. This testimony forms the heart of this report. National studies and professional articles are also cited, as well as surveys of local high school students' attitudes about gay and lesbian youth issues.

The first half of the report discusses the problems encountered by gay and lesbian students in school as well as the problems of their family members. The report outlines these problems in the following five sections:

1. "Harassment of Gay and Lesbian Students in School"
2. "Isolation and Suicide"
3. "Drop-Out and Poor School Performance"
4. "Gay and Lesbian Youth and Their Need for Adult Role Models"
5. "Families of Gay and Lesbian Youth"

Recommendations to schools

In the second half of the report, the Commission makes a series of recommendations directly to schools about how to make Massachusetts school environments safe for gay and lesbian students and how to help these young people realize their educational potential. The Commission urges Governor Weld, the Department of Education, and the Executive Office of Education to endorse these recommendations and to devise a plan for their implementation throughout the Commonwealth.

Five specific recommendations to schools are in the following areas:

1. School policies protecting gay and lesbian students from harassment, violence, and discrimination.
2. Training teachers, counselors, and school staff in crisis intervention and violence prevention.
3. School-based support groups for gay and straight students.
4. Information in school libraries for gay and lesbian adolescents.
5. Curriculum which includes gay and lesbian issues.

The Commission makes three recommendations for helping families of gay and lesbian youth:

1. Peer counselling in the P-FLAG (Parents and Friends of Lesbians and Gays) model and family counselling in school.
2. Education of families through information in public libraries.
3. Parent speakers bureaus to advocate for fair treatment of gay and lesbian youth in schools.

Recommendations to state agencies and the legislature

To facilitate both implementation of its recommendations in local schools and to educate teachers, school personnel, families, and students about the problems of gay and lesbian teenagers, the Commission makes recommendations to three state agencies: the Department of Education, the Executive Office of Education, and the Massachusetts Commission Against Discrimination (MCAD). The Commission also endorses legislation for the Massachusetts Legislature to enact.

The Commission's three recommendations to the Department of Education are:

1. Sponsor training for teachers, families, and students to learn about the problems of gay and lesbian youth.
2. Make presentations to school committee associations concerning the problems faced by gay and lesbian youth.
3. Develop and disseminate a yellow pages resource book about gay and lesbian youth, one version each for students, teachers, and families.

The Commission's three recommendations to the Executive Office of Education focus on policies and research:

1. Develop and promote anti-harassment policies and guidelines for protecting gay and lesbian students in schools across the Commonwealth.
2. Develop school policies that will guarantee gay and lesbian students equal rights to an education and equal access to school activities.
3. Research the problems of gay and lesbian students, and the needs of teachers and families of gay and lesbian youth.

The state's leading civil rights agency, the Massachusetts Commission Against Discrimination (MCAD), is urged to do the following three things:

1. Conduct outreach to teachers and school personnel to inform them of their rights under the state's Gay and Lesbian Civil Rights Law, which was enacted in 1989.
2. Sponsor anti-discrimination awareness programs in schools for all students to learn about the gay and lesbian civil rights law.
3. Sponsor legislation to extend MCAD's jurisdiction to include complaints of education discrimination.

Finally, the Massachusetts legislature is urged to enact, and Governor Weld urged to prioritize passage of, legislation protecting gay and lesbian students in public schools against discrimination in admission to schools or access to school activities and courses of study.

INTRODUCTION

"We feel strongly that there is a tremendous need to address the difficult issues facing gay and lesbian youth. Half a million young people attempt suicide every year. Nearly 30% of youth suicides are committed by gays or lesbians ... We must abolish the prejudice and isolation faced by gay and lesbian youth. We need to help them stay at home and stay in school so they can have healthy and productive lives."
—Governor William Weld, speaking at the swearing-in ceremony for the members of the Governor's Commission on Gay and Lesbian Youth on June 11, 1992.

History of the formation of the nation's first Governor's Commission on Gay and Lesbian Youth

The Governor's Commission on Gay and Lesbian Youth had its origins as a bill that was written by the Coalition for Lesbian and Gay Civil Rights in late 1989, immediately following the legislature's passage of the Gay and Lesbian Civil Rights Law. The Coalition for Lesbian and Gay Civil Rights filed legislation to create an advisory board focusing on gay and lesbian youth services. Representative Alvin Thompson (D-Cambridge) was the chief sponsor of the bill.

The legislation was refiled for the 1991 legislative session and came to the attention of the media on May 7, 1991, when Lieutenant Governor Paul Cellucci publicly endorsed the bill on behalf of himself and Governor William Weld. The bill passed the House in December, 1991, but died in the Senate at the close of the session.

Governor Weld at that point offered to create a commission by executive order; the Commission would last throughout his administration. The order was drafted by the Coalition for Lesbian and Gay Civil Rights in consultation with the Weld administration. The executive order broadened the mandate of the original legislation considerably.

On February 10, 1992, Governor William F. Weld and Lieutenant Governor Paul Cellucci signed an executive order creating the Governor's Commission on Gay and Lesbian Youth. The Commission is the first of its kind in the United States. On June 11, 1992, Governor Weld swore in the 27 members of the Commission, including two high school students, two parents of gay and lesbian children, three teachers, and a number of human services professionals. Governor Weld urged the Commission to gather information and hold public hearings and to submit a report to him within a year.

U.S. report on gay and lesbian youth suicide brings the issue to public awareness

> "Adolescent suicide attempts result from the adolescent feeling that he has been subject to a progressive isolation from meaningful social relationships, because of problems that he/she felt to be 'unshareable.'"   —J. Jacobs (Adolescent Suicide, 1971)

In 1989, the United States Department of Health and Human Services issued a stunning report on youth suicide, with a chapter on gay and lesbian youth suicide. Pressure from anti-gay forces within the Bush/Quayle administration led to suppression, not only of the controversial chapter, but also of the entire report. Only 3000 copies of the report were printed and little or no action was taken to deal with the epidemic of youth suicide, let alone the problems of gay and lesbian adolescents. Statistics in the report revealed that between 1950 and 1980, the suicide rate for youths aged 15 through 24 rose 170% as opposed to only 20% for the total population. This clearly indicated an alarming rise in the suicide rate for all youth.

Even more striking was the fact that gay and lesbian youth accounted for approximately *one-third of all youth suicides*. Five hundred thousand young people attempt suicide annually; of these, gay and lesbian youth are two to three times more likely to attempt suicide than their heterosexual peers. The report also revealed that suicide is the leading cause of death among gay and lesbian youth.

Commission mandate

Alarmed by the findings of this report, both members of the gay and lesbian community as well as health professionals began to call for greater efforts to meet the needs of gay and lesbian youth. Governor William Weld expressed his support for this initiative through the creation of the Commission and in a personal appearance at the swearing-in of Commission members. At this event, Governor Weld urged the Commission to make curbing the high rate of suicide among gay and lesbian youth its top priority. "We feel strongly that there is a tremendous need to address the difficult issues facing gay and lesbian youth," said Governor Weld at the ceremony. "Half a million young people attempt suicide every year. Nearly 30% of youth suicides are committed by gays or lesbians ... We must abolish the prejudice and isolation faced by gay and lesbian youth. We need to help them stay at home and stay in school so they can have healthy and productive lives."

According to the executive order, the Commission has a broad mandate. Preventing suicide and preventing violence against gay and lesbian youth are its priorities, and it is also charged with working to end all forms of discrimination against youth who are gay or lesbian. The Commission reports directly to the Governor, meets regularly with three of his cabinet secretaries, and makes recommendations to both public and private agencies about creation of policies and programs to help gay and lesbian youth.

The Commission is active on an ongoing basis, serving under the Weld/Cellucci administration. In the first six months of its existence, Commission members have launched a statewide campaign to educate the public of Massachusetts about the problems of gay and lesbian youth. Commission members have made a variety of public appearances, speaking to teachers, human service professionals, youth, and family groups, both in person and through the media.

The Commission's Public Hearings: A voice for gay and lesbian youth

In the fall of 1992, the Commission held a series of five public hearings to gather testimony from gay and lesbian youth, from teachers, from parents of gays and lesbians, and [from] human service professionals. The testimony from these hearings forms the heart of this report. An unprecedented number of gay and lesbian youth spoke out at these hearings, which were widely covered by the mainstream print media, by radio, and [by] television. The result was to put a human face on the suffering of gay and lesbian youth and to bring their personal stories to the attention of Massachusetts citizens.

The hearings were statewide and offered regional diversity. The first hearing was held in Amherst on November 13 and the second was held in Worcester on November 16. The two largest hearings were held at the State House on November 17 and November 18. The final hearing was in Springfield on December 1. A total of 90 people testified at these hearings.

The hearings, in addition to providing the testimony for this report, also crystallized the mission of the Governor's Commission on Gay and Lesbian Youth. The Commission is committed to giving an ongoing voice to gay and lesbian youth, a voice in their schools, in their families and communities, and a voice in the media through the young people who have chosen to speak out publicly. The courage, honesty, and pride of these young gays and lesbians continue to broaden public support and understanding for our work.

Identifying the problems of gay and lesbian youth

At the hearings and through our research, the Commission found that gay and lesbian youth face numerous, often unendurable, obstacles growing up gay or lesbian in this society. Gay and lesbian youth exist in a society that in attitude and behavior discriminates against them. Society at large creates a mythology about gays and lesbians, and virtually denies the existence of gay and lesbian youth. Parents, family, peers, and teachers are generally ignorant of what it means to be gay or lesbian. Gay and lesbian youth have little chance of talking with a knowledgeable or understanding person concerning his or her gay or lesbian identity.

Overt hostility, in addition to ignorance and silence, surrounds gay and lesbian youth. Both adults and peers often reject gay and lesbian youths. This often takes the form of physical violence and verbal harassment, leading 28% of gay and lesbian youth to drop out of high school, according to the U.S. Department of Health and Human Services. The primary effects of society's hostility and lack of acceptance are feelings of isolation, extreme low self-esteem, and consequent attempts at self-destructive behavior.

An unsafe environment in school

Inspired by the testimony of these youth, the Commission has chosen to first focus on schools, where the prevailing unsafe climate denies equal educational opportunity to lesbian and gay youth. Virtually every youth who testified before the Commission cited the need for action to change their school environment. Often the first-person experiences these youth related were horrifying — stories of violence, abuse, and harassment, from both peers and adults. Given that state government has a responsibility to guarantee equal opportunity and a safe environment for all the students in the Commonwealth's schools, the Commission has focused its first report around recommendations designed to create an environment where all students might learn, free from fear and intimidation.

"Making Schools Safe for Gay and Lesbian Youth"

This report, entitled "Making Schools Safe for Gay and Lesbian Youth," is the first in a series of reports the Commission will issue. It outlines the problems faced by gay and lesbian youth in school and makes a series of recommendations that seek to guarantee safety and end abuse. Massachusetts Public Schools need to abolish abuse, harassment, and violence against these youth. In addition, schools must provide support through school-based gay/straight student groups, from counselors and teachers, and through information in school libraries.

School, along with family, forms the life of the teenager. It is within the purview of state government to set guidelines, and work to promote school policies and programs on a statewide basis to make schools safe for gay and lesbian youth. This report is the first step in meeting the obligation our government has to guarantee equal educational opportunity and safety for all of its youth.

Note: For the sake of format consistency, the Commission has chosen to use the phrase "gay and lesbian youth" to describe all youth who suffer from prejudice based on sexual identity. In reality, however, this term is meant to be inclusive of not only gay and lesbian youth but also those who self-identify as bisexual, those whose dress does not conform to gender expectations, those who are themselves heterosexual but have gay and lesbian family members, or those who are simply perceived by others to be gay or lesbian.

I. HARASSMENT OF GAY AND LESBIAN STUDENTS IN SCHOOL

"I just began hating myself more and more, as each year, the hatred towards me grew and escalated from just simple name-calling in elementary school to having persons in high school threaten to beat me up, being pushed and dragged around on the ground, having hands slammed in lockers, and a number of other daily tortures."

—Steven Obuchowski, 18, testifying at the Governor's Commission on Gay and Lesbian Youth's Public Hearings.

"Last year at my high school, there was an incident which shocked everyone. Two female students were standing in the hall with their arms around each other. Students began to encircle them and yell profanities, until a group of about thirty kids surrounded them."

—Zoe Hart, 17, senior at Lincoln-Sudbury High School, testifying at the Public Hearings.

Gay and lesbian youth report that they are subjected to a wide range of verbal and physical abuse in school from other students and sometimes even from teachers. This abuse can be delivered in many forms, ranging from derogatory slurs to violent beatings. School for these young men and women is far from being a safe place.

At the Governor's Commission on Gay and Lesbian Youth's Public Hearings, young gays and lesbians gave testimony about the terrorizing anti-gay violence that they face in their schools.

"We were picked on. We were called 'queer' and 'faggot' and a host of other homophobic slurs. We were also used as punching bags by our classmates, just for being different." —Chris Muther, 23, testifying at the Public Hearings about himself and his friend, Richard, who later committed suicide.

"I was very different from the other students and everyone picked up on it. Immediately the words 'faggot' and 'queer' were used to describe me. In Wareham, being anything but a cool jock is socially unacceptable." —Randy Driskell, 18, senior at Wareham High School, testifying at the Public Hearings.

"At Eaglebrook, homophobia and hazing were rampant. I had to be adamantly heterosexual and had to make dehumanizing comments about girls or else be labelled a faggot. I had to prove my masculinity by hazing the underclassmen. Others found pushing wasn't enough and so turned to whiffle-ball bats. Once someone was rolled down cement steps in a laundry bag just for the fun of it." —Devin Beringer, 17, senior at Concord Academy, testifying at the Public Hearings.

Nearly half of gay men and one in five lesbians are harassed or assaulted in secondary school

A survey of 2,074 gay adults conducted by the National Gay and Lesbian Task Force in 1984 found that 45% of the males and 20% of the females reported having experienced verbal or physical assaults in secondary school because they were perceived to be gay or lesbian.

"One of my best friends ... was only suspected of being gay. He was not, as a matter of fact. But at that suspicion, only that suspicion, he was beaten up every day at school. He was unable to attend classes many days." —Chris Collins, University of Massachusetts–Amherst student, testifying at the Public Hearings.

Violence against gay and lesbian students in school is part of an increasing incidence of violence against gays and lesbians in the world at large.

The most frequent victims of hate violence today are blacks, Hispanics, Southeast Asians, Jews, and gays and lesbians. Homosexuals are probably the most frequent victims. —U.S. Justice Department (*The Response of the Criminal Justice System to Bias Crime: An Exploratory View,* 1987).

Massachusetts enacted the Hate Crimes Reporting Act in 1990, which provides for training of police and collection of statistics about hate crimes directed against gays and lesbians, blacks, Jews, and other minorities. However, the protection afforded adults by this law has yet to be extended to our schools.

97% of students surveyed at Lincoln-Sudbury Regional High School report hearing anti-gay comments in school

In Massachusetts, a survey designed by the Governor's Commission on Gay and Lesbian Youth was distributed to all students at Lincoln-Sudbury Regional High School in February of 1993. Three hundred ninety-eight male and female students responded to the survey. Students were asked the question "How often have you heard homophobic remarks made at your school?" An overwhelming 97.5% of the respondents said they had heard homophobic remarks at school. Forty-nine percent of the students reported they had heard the remarks very often and 49% had heard the remarks sometimes. Only 2.5% had never heard anti-gay comments in school.

Lack of school policies to prevent anti-gay harassment

Only a handful of schools in Massachusetts have policies which protect students against anti-gay harassment; few school administrations discipline students for name-calling and harassment of gay and lesbian students.

> Schools do not adequately protect gay youth, with teachers often reluctant to stop harassment or rebut homophobic remarks. —Paul Gibson, U.S. Department of Health and Human Services (*Report of the Secretary's Task Force on Youth Suicide,* 1989).

Gay and lesbian students, required by law like their peers to attend public schools, find themselves in a dangerous, unsafe environment day after day, yet despite their vulnerability, policies are not in place and teacher-training has not been undertaken to ensure their safety.

> "I have spoken to teachers in schools on the issue of name-calling in the hallways and they feel they are not justified in going up to students in the hallways and saying, 'You cannot use that word.' And I ask them, if someone called an African-American student a nigger, would you stand around in your classroom and say, 'It's not my place to go out.'?" —Sharon Bergman, 18, testifying at the Public Hearings.

Sometimes teachers and school personnel, in addition to students, are abusive towards gay and lesbian students. Dorothy Remur, the mother of a gay son, testified that when her son Douglas came out as gay in his senior year at Dedham High School, he faced hostility from teachers as well as students.

> "The young women often caught one of the male gym teachers walking with the jocks of the school and the teacher was making

derogatory hand signals towards Douglas. I realize that children can be very cruel, but when teachers and adults encourage or do not discourage mean and cruel behavior it makes me angry and very sad."
—Dorothy Remur, mother of a gay son, testifying at the Public Hearings.

Teachers may wish to stop harassment and anti-gay comments, yet they lack the backing of administration. Few teachers have had specific training which would teach them to intervene effectively, and many fear reprisals without the explicit support and backing of their administration. Consequently, gay and lesbian youth bashing continues in our schools.

Abuse of gay and lesbian youth and suicide attempts

The messages gay and lesbian youth receive about themselves from homophobic peers and teachers are devastating. The hatred others inflict on them is often turned into self-hatred. The violence others unleash on them is often echoed in acts of self-destruction. Joyce Hunter of the Hetrick-Martin Institute, a community-based agency in New York City that provides services for gay and lesbian youth, emphasizes how abuse of these youth puts them at risk for suicide.

Violence towards youths is also believed to be associated with violence towards oneself, manifested in the form of suicidal behavior.
—Joyce Hunter ("Violence against Lesbian and Gay Male Youths," 1990).

In 1988, Hunter surveyed violence-victimization and self-destructive behavior among 500 self-identified gay and lesbian youth. Forty-one percent of these youths reported that they had experienced violent attacks, many at the hands of classmates. Forty-six percent of the violence against these young people was gay-related. Suicidal ideation was found among 44% of those gay and lesbian youth who had experienced violent assaults.

The harassment and violence encountered by many gay and lesbian youth in schools interferes with their right to a safe and complete education. In the worst-case scenario, the threatening school environment can be a contributing factor to suicide or attempted suicide by gay and lesbian youth.

II. ISOLATION AND SUICIDE

"I felt as though I was the only gay person my age in the world. I felt as though I had nowhere to go to talk to anybody. Throughout eighth grade, I went to bed every night praying that I would not be able to wake up in the morning, and every morning waking up and being disappointed. And so finally I decided that if I was going to die, it would have to be at my own hands."
          —Steven Obuchowski, 18, testifying at the Public Hearings.

Steve Obuchowski tried to kill himself while attending a school that had no support group for gay and lesbian students and no counselling or referrals available. His belief that dying was the only way out of his isolation is a common one among gay and lesbian teens.

Gay and lesbian youth report that by junior high and high school they experienced intense feelings of aloneness in school. Often their isolation and pain is misunderstood by adults.

"Due to societal fear and ignorance, my teachers and counselors labelled my confusion as rebellion and placed me in the category of a troubled discipline problem. But still I had nothing to identify with and no role models to guide me, to help me sort out this confusion, and I began to believe that I was simply alone ... A few weeks into my sophomore year, I woke up in a psych hospital in Brookline after taking my father's camping knife violently to my wrists and hoping for success." —Stacey Harris, Curry College student, testifying at the Public Hearings.

Stacey Harris, like Steve Obuchowski, made suicide attempts while attending high schools that had no support groups, nor any counselling, for gay and lesbian students.

Suicide among gay and lesbian youth

Suicide is the leading cause of death for gay and lesbian adolescents, according to the 1989 *Report of the Secretary's Task Force on Youth Suicide* (U.S. Department of Health and Human Services, Gibson). The Federal study on youth suicide states:
   • There is an epidemic of youth suicide in the United States today.
   • 500,000 youths try to kill themselves each year.

- Between 1950 and 1980, there was a 170% increase in suicides of people between the ages of 15 and 24.
- Gay and lesbian youth are 2 to 3 times more likely to attempt suicide than their peers.
- Gay and lesbian youth comprise 30% of completed youth suicides.

Lack of school-based support groups for gay and lesbian students in all but a few of Massachusetts public schools leaves the young gay or lesbian person alone with his or her feelings of difference at a time of life when acceptance from a peer group is so important. Many of the adolescents testifying at the Governor's Commission on Gay and Lesbian Youth's Public Hearings described feelings of profound isolation in school.

> "I was always an outcast at school. Books were my best friends. I ostracized myself from the rest of the world because I felt as if I could trust no one, not even my parents. The pressure of feeling so alone manifested itself in fits of manic depression, hysterical outbreaks, and, eventually, suicidal tendencies." —Devin Beringer, 17, senior at Concord Academy, testifying at the Public Hearings.

> "I couldn't see or find a community of people like me and so I felt I had no home anywhere, no place to relax and be myself." —Lee Fearnside, 18, testifying at the Public Hearings.

The pervasive name-calling and threats of anti-gay harassment in school force many students to further isolate themselves from their classmates in order to protect their safety. Dorothy Remur, the mother of a gay son, described her son's aloneness in school.

> "One of the teachers told me how the other children treated my son. She told me how they pushed and shoved him, knocking the books out of his hands. Douglas made a point to walk through the hallways after the final bell so they were almost empty. This was to protect himself." —Dorothy Remur, parent, testifying at the Public Hearings.

Schools become places where gay and lesbian students feel cut off from their heterosexual peers, as well as from teachers, counselors, and administrators. Students in rural areas, far from any signs of a visible gay/lesbian community, often feel even more alone.

"On the Cape where I live, there is nothing for gay and lesbian youth. I knew something had to be done, but I didn't know what." —Randy Driskell, 18, senior at Wareham High School, testifying at the Public Hearings.

Marilyn C. McManus writes of the isolation young gays and lesbians experience in rural schools.

They experience the same pressures urban gay and lesbian youth face. These stresses are, however, exacerbated for rural youth. They are geographically isolated and are even less likely to find supportive role models than their urban peers. Rural youth have a more difficult time identifying peers struggling with sexual orientation issues, lack access to support networks, and are less likely ... to find gay-positive materials in their libraries or schools. —Marilyn C. McManus ("Serving Gay and Lesbian Youth," 1991).

In addition to the lack of peer support and acceptance at school, many of the gay and lesbian youth testifying at the Public Hearings reported a lack of accurate information about who gays and lesbians really are. Gay and lesbian students also reported a lack of information about resources for gay and lesbian youth.

"I went to Boston English High. There was no literature in the school at all. The guidance counselor wouldn't even recommend BAGLY (the Boston Alliance of Gay and Lesbian Youth)." —Anthony Flynn, testifying at the Public Hearings.

Low self-esteem and risk for suicide

The negative views about gays and lesbians so commonly expressed by students in class, in the halls, and during school activities teach the lesbian or gay adolescent to develop a negative self-image. With no one to talk to and with pervasive abuse, school becomes, not a place of self-actualization, but a place where the young gay or lesbian person learns to hate himself/herself.

"But who could I talk to? Through the last few years, I had been conditioned into believing gay is wrong ... After three years of conditioning, I forgot all the things my mother taught me. I lost respect for myself and wanted to die." —Randy Driskell, 18, testifying at the Public Hearings.

"I felt completely isolated from my family and friends. It appeared that I was the only one who ever had these queer feelings. I couldn't come out to anyone. After all, who would associate with anyone who was sick and deranged as I thought myself to be if they knew the truth. Not only does society shout at me that I am evil, but an inner voice whispers it as well." —Lee Fearnside, 18, testifying at the Public Hearings.

Doctor John T. Maltsberger, one of the country's leading experts on suicide, reports that self-hatred, low self-esteem, and intense feelings of aloneness are typical of the profile of a suicidal person.

In the grips of aloneness the patient is convinced he will be forever cut off from the possibility of human connectedness; in suicidal worthlessness, the patient is convinced he can never merit the caring notice of anyone, including himself, again. The subjective result is the same: to be beyond love is to be hopelessly alone. —John Maltsberger (*Suicide Risk: The Formulation of Clinical Judgment,* 1986).

"What school support gives kids is life."

Many students at the Governor's Commission Public Hearings testified that suicide attempts by gay and lesbian youth might be prevented if support were available at school.

"I think if I was made more aware of support groups for young gay and lesbian people — I really had no idea at all of any support groups — and if people were a lot more compassionate, then I think that things may have been different, and perhaps I could have led a more normal life." —Steve Obuchowski, 18, testifying at the Public Hearings.

"I never slashed, I never swallowed, I never jumped; I was much luckier than some of the people that we have heard today. As different as each episode was, the reasons for stopping short were the same. Every time, I was able to call on someone from the Concord Academy Gay/Straight Alliance, or someone who I'd come out to through the strength and support I received there, and call out for help." —Sharon Bergman, 18, testifying at the Public Hearings.

Devin Beringer, who is currently a senior at Concord Academy, also believes that having a support group in school and sympathetic people to talk with made the difference in his life.

"I've spent more than one lonely night sobbing while downing shot after shot, and I've also planned out my suicide more than once. Fortunately I was not alone. There were gay students and gay faculty to whom I could go for help." —Devin Beringer, 17, testifying at the Public Hearings.

Reluctance on the part of the vast majority of schools to encourage discussions of gay and lesbian issues for students and faculty perpetuates the isolation and loneliness of lesbian/gay teens that so often drives them to attempt suicide. Unfortunately for far too many young people, fear of these discussions continues to prevent schools from being able to take the steps necessary to create a supportive environment for all students.

"That is the first step: when the teachers and the principals and the superintendents are not afraid, then the students are not afraid. And when the students are not afraid, they will live. The question is not a matter of a smoother high school experience. What school support gives kids is life." —Sharon Bergman, 18, testifying at the Public Hearings.

60% of students surveyed at Lincoln-Sudbury High School think high schools should have groups for gay and lesbian students

In Massachusetts, a survey designed by the Governor's Commission on Gay and Lesbian Youth was distributed to all students at Lincoln-Sudbury Regional High School in February of 1993.

Three hundred ninety-eight students responded to the survey. When asked the question "Do you think high schools should have groups or clubs that support gay, lesbian, and bisexual students?" 60% of the students answered "Yes," with 20% answering "No" and 18% undecided.

III. DROP-OUT AND POOR SCHOOL PERFORMANCE

"During junior high and in my freshman year of high school, I was very depressed. Feeling alone and isolated from the rest of the world, I managed to fail three of my five majors that year."
—Matthew Flynn, 18, testifying at the Public Hearings.

"I suggested (to my father) that maybe I was failing because I am uncomfortable in school and avoid it as much as possible."
—James Cohen, 15, student at the Commonwealth School in the Back Bay, testifying at the Public Hearings.

For many gay and lesbian students, school is not a place of learning, but a place where they feel profoundly isolated, sometimes even suicidal; a place where they are abused and terrorized by violence for being different. The U.S. Department of Health and Human Services reports that gay and lesbian students often have their right to an education jeopardized because of the hostility of the school environment.

The shame of ridicule and fear of attacks makes school a fearful place to go, resulting in frequent absences and sometimes academic failure.
—Paul Gibson, U.S. Department of Health and Human Services (*Report of the Secretary's Task Force on Youth Suicide,* 1989).

"My attendance at school has fallen steadily and school has become a place I no longer want to be, mostly, I feel, because of the lack of education and acceptance of diversity, but more so, the homophobia among faculty and students." —Adelaide Goetz, 16, junior at Cambridge Rindge and Latin High School, testifying at the Public Hearings.

Alienation from school activities

In addition to experiencing academic difficulties, many gay and lesbian students report that hostility from their peers threatens their ability to participate in school activities such as athletics and social events.

Dorothy Remur testified of her gay son's difficulties in gym class.

"They (the school administration) told me that the gym class Douglas was attending consisted of a very tough group of boys, and they teased and tormented him terribly. The teacher couldn't control their behav-

ior, so the only solution was to excuse Doug from the class. I requested that he be placed in another class. This never happened."
—Dorothy Remur, parent, testifying at the Public Hearings.

"Things had escalated where during gym class people would shove food and gum and other objects inside my clothing during the gym class." —Steven Obuchowski, 18, testifying at the Public Hearings.

"Basketball has been the love of my life since I was a young child and I could never imagine not playing. But recently, the thoughts of not going out for the team have been very strong. I have spent the last two years ignoring homophobic comments during the season." —Adelaide Goetz, 16, testifying at the Public Hearings.

60% of students surveyed at Lincoln-Sudbury Regional High School would be afraid or upset if people thought they were gay, lesbian, or bisexual

In Massachusetts, a survey designed by the Governor's Commission on Gay and Lesbian Youth was distributed to all students at Lincoln-Sudbury Regional High School in February of 1993. Three hundred ninety-eight students responded to the survey. Students were asked the question "Would you be upset or afraid if people thought you were gay, lesbian, or bisexual?" Sixty percent of the students said "Yes," 22% didn't know how they would feel, and only 18% said "No."

Students were also asked the question "How would your friends react to finding out someone they knew was gay, lesbian, or bisexual?" Thirty-four percent of the students thought their friends would be uncomfortable if they found out someone they knew was gay, lesbian, or bisexual; an additional 10% said they thought their friends would stop being friends with the person. Only 15% of the students said they thought their friends would be supportive of a gay or lesbian acquaintance, with 20% saying their friends would be indifferent and 21% being unsure of the reaction.

Fear, rejection, and the high drop-out rate of gay and lesbian students

In many cases, feelings of alienation in classes and in school activities combined with hostility from peers make gay and lesbian adolescents unable to complete their high school education. The 1989 *Report of the Secretary's Task Force on Youth Suicide* estimates that 28% of gay and lesbian youth drop out of school because of discomfort in the school environment.

Troix Bettencourt concealed his homosexuality from the other students at Lowell High School. He was popular, and engaged in many school activities. Yet the internal strain led to an inability to continue in school.

"I couldn't handle being in high school living something that I wasn't, so I just dropped out and I just called it quits and I just couldn't handle it anymore. I thought about suicide and I thought about leaving home because I just couldn't handle it anymore." —Troix Bettencourt, 18, testifying at the Public Hearings.

Randy Driskell reports being driven out of high school because of constant verbal abuse and violence.

"I was spit on, pushed, and ridiculed. My school life was hell. I decided to leave school because I couldn't handle it." —Randy Driskell, 18, testifying at the Public Hearings.

Dropping out of school combines with other stresses in the lives of gay and lesbian adolescents. Many face real or imagined rejection from family, and a growing sense of having no place of belonging or acceptance. Though some gay and lesbian youth manage to return to school after finding a supportive adult, many wind up on the streets, out of school and out of a home.

The U.S. Department of Health and Human Services estimates that at any given time, gay and lesbian adolescents comprise a substantial percentage of street youth.

Gay male, lesbian, bisexual, and transsexual youth comprise as many as 25% of all youth living on the streets in this country. Here, they enter a further outcast status that presents serious dangers and even greater risk for suicide. Without an adequate education or vocational training, many are forced to become involved in prostitution in order to survive. —Paul Gibson, U.S. Department of Health and Human Services (*Report of the Secretary's Task Force on Youth Suicide,* 1989).

Suicide attempts and disruption of high school education

The frequency of suicide attempts by gay and lesbian youth is another factor which severely disrupts their education. The turmoil, hospitalization, and physical problems in the aftermath of suicide attempts can delay and often prevent successful completion of class-work and graduation from high school.

> "I was placed in thirteen hospitals in two years. By what was supposed to be my junior year of high school, I had accumulated a resume consisting of five suicide attempts, two bottles of pills, four half-way houses, several high schools, and one family in shock. They (the doctors) told me I would never graduate high school." —Stacey Harris, Curry College student, testifying at the Public Hearings.

Tragic patterns of unhappiness and alienation in school, of being prevented from attending classes or enjoying school activities, of being driven to drop out or to attempt suicide: these all occur during the critical period of adolescent learning and intellectual growth. For far too many of our gay and lesbian youth, the fundamental right to an education is being taken away.

IV. GAY AND LESBIAN YOUTH AND THEIR NEED FOR ADULT ROLE MODELS

> *"If not for the support I found in openly gay teachers at my high school, I would be dead today. I hope to God that future teach-ers have the courage to come out for their students."*
> —Sharon Bergman, 18, testifying at the Public Hearings.

> *"In the schools I went to, homosexuality was there, but it was never talked about. You were made to feel in school that you were different, that you were disgusting."*
> —Steve Wilson, testifying at the Public Hearings.

Adults set the tone of the school community. Through both explicit and implicit means, they send messages to students about what sorts of attitudes, behavior, and conduct are acceptable. Adults who work in Massachusetts schools are ill-equipped to meet the needs of lesbian and gay students. Either intimidated or ignorant, school staffs often fail to provide these young people with the support and even with the protection they need.

At the Public Hearings of the Governor's Commission on Gay and Lesbian Youth, many gay and lesbian adolescents spoke of their need for positive adult role models in school. Students who were fortunate enough to have such role models testified about the benefits.

"I was constantly denying the feelings I had for other guys. In the process of hiding these feelings, I repressed all emotions. Concord Academy changed all this. It was the first place I encountered that was even slightly gay-positive. When I arrived, an openly gay faculty member was assigned to be my advisor. Through him, I learned that being gay is not the horrible and disgusting thing society makes it out to be, but instead, a normal and natural part of me." —Devin Beringer, 17, testifying at the Public Hearings.

Studies such as those by Professor Gregory Herek of the University of California–Davis have shown that the key factor in reducing fear and intolerance of gays and lesbians is a positive personal experience with an openly gay or lesbian person (Herek, 1985). The presence of openly gay/lesbian staff members is a crucial component of any school program seeking to reduce bigotry and provide support for lesbian and gay students. However, the vast majority of youth attend schools with no openly gay or lesbian personnel.

Hostility towards gay and lesbian youth on the part of school staff

Often teachers and school personnel, in addition to being unresponsive to the needs of gay and lesbian students, will themselves be overtly hostile to these young people and use derogatory language about gays and lesbians.

"An administrator in my school, after a particularly embarrassing episode, used in her defense, 'Well, you must have AIDS. You're gay, aren't you?' She didn't realize how much that hurt." —James Cohen, 15, testifying at the Public Hearings.

Arthur Lipkin, who taught for twenty years at Cambridge Rindge and Latin High School, testified about an incident of verbal abuse by an adult staff member.

"I was standing at one end of a corridor and at the other end two male students were wrestling, just horsing around, I guess. I saw the school security person approach these two boys. She bellowed at them, 'Break it up, you homos!' The corridor echoed with her words and I was horrified. I challenged her on the spot and she replied bitterly, 'I wasn't talking to you.'" —Arthur Lipkin, teacher, testifying at the Public Hearings.

Research by Professor James Sears of the University of South Carolina showed that 8 out of 10 teachers in training harbored anti-gay attitudes. Fully one-third were rated as 'high-grade homophobes,' using a classification system designed to reveal the depth of anti-gay feelings (Sears, 1989). The chilling effect of such adult bigotry on gay and lesbian youth is self-evident.

Teachers fear supporting gay and lesbian students

An atmosphere of intolerance in the schools intimidates gay and lesbian teachers into remaining closeted, thus denying students role models they need. Gay and lesbian teachers testifying at the Governor's Commission on Gay and Lesbian Youth's Public Hearings spoke of being afraid they would be harassed, dismissed, or even physically attacked if they were open about being gay or lesbian in school.

Maryanne Jennings, an English teacher in the Springfield Public Schools for the past 21 years, testified about her fears concerning becoming known in her school as a lesbian teacher.

"Today in school it's okay to hate gays and lesbians; it's actually encouraged by the behaviors and attitudes of faculty and staff. It's not a safe environment. I have not felt safe since my face was on television a few weeks ago on the *20/20* segment on lesbians. In fact, in my school I've experienced an awful lot of harassment in the weeks since then." —Maryanne Jennings, teacher, testifying at the Public Hearings.

Unfortunately, research studies and anecdotal evidence both suggest that teachers' fears are not misplaced. A study by University of South Carolina Professor James Sears found that the majority of school administrators surveyed said they would indeed fire a teacher whom they knew to be gay or lesbian (Harbeck, 1992).

Gay and lesbian students suffer because of the silence and fears of their teachers. The young gay or lesbian person's experience of isolation worsens through sensing the shame and invisibility on the part of adults in the school. Kathy Henderson, the co-director of the Gay and Lesbian School Teachers Network (GLISTN) and a teacher at Phillips Academy (Andover), says fear prevents teachers from protecting students against anti-gay harassment.

"Most teachers, gay or straight, are afraid to speak up when they hear homophobic remarks. They feel it might put them at risk, that people might say, 'What are you — gay?' which remains a frightening question for most teachers to answer in the current climate." —Kathy Henderson, teacher, testimony submitted to the Governor's Commission.

The experience of Robert Cornigans, a gay African-American English teacher, is a case study of what many teachers fear would happen if they tried to help their students by standing up to anti-gay bigotry. In 1988, Mr. Cornigans was hired as a substitute teacher at a private school.

"I can see I was hired in mid-October to fill one niche in his quest for diversity, and fired in mid-December because my being gay represented a niche that was too diverse for him to handle." —Robert Cornigans, testimony submitted to the Governor's Commission.

Cornigans originally had no intention of being open about being gay, but events put him in a difficult position.

"One of my freshman students ... confronted me with an essay, the essence of which suggested all gays should be hung ... Perhaps I shouldn't have said anything to 'Matthew,' and held my tongue as I had done so many times in the past, but I didn't. 'You can't,' a voice inside me said, 'because here's a kid who needs someone to help him.' So I said ... 'I'm gay.' ... A few weeks later I let another student who asked me about my girlfriend know I was gay by showing him a letter (nothing of an erotic nature) I'd written to my boyfriend. That was the extent of my conversations with either boy about homosexuality." —Robert Cornigans.

About a week later, the headmaster told Cornigans he was dismissed because he'd "ruined the boys' lives." Most of the student body and many faculty members petitioned the headmaster to reconsider his position, but he would not.

The Massachusetts Gay and Lesbian Civil Rights Law, which passed in 1989, protects teachers, as well as other workers, against employment discrimination based on sexual orientation. Yet few schools in their faculty handbooks or in teacher contracts explicitly make a commitment to enforcing equal rights protection for gay and lesbian faculty. The fear of discrimination on the part of adults in school remains pervasive, extending even beyond those who really are gay or lesbian.

> Heterosexual professionals also face pressures. Like their lesbian or gay colleagues, they may fear that nondiscriminatory work for lesbian and gay adolescents would open them to the charge of "promoting homosexuality." The school climate is fraught with risks. —Joyce Hunter ("Stresses on Lesbian and Gay Adolescents in Schools," 1987).

Several teachers who spoke at the Public Hearings, however, testified about how they were able to overcome their fears and begin to serve as role models for their students. Robert Parlin, a teacher at Newton South High School, cites two issues that motivated him to take the step to come out to his students:

> "First, I began to think about the terrible messages that closeted gay teachers send to their students: that being gay is shameful, not an appropriate subject for discussion; that lesbians and gay men were not welcome or valued members of the school community; and second, I received tremendous support and encouragement from my principal, my department chair, and a large group of faculty members." — Robert Parlin, testifying at the Public Hearings.

Parlin testified about the positive effect being honest with his students had on his teaching.

> "My students responded with thoughtfulness, compassion, and sincere respect. Many came up to me later that day to tell me how much they admired what I had done and how it had changed their way of thinking about gay people ... The reverse of my fears occurred. I actually became closer to my students as a result of coming out." —Robert Parlin.

Only a few public schools in Massachusetts have made a commitment to protecting and upholding the rights of gay and lesbian teachers and others wishing to provide support for lesbian/gay students. Most school environments continue to remain as threatening for the adult staff as they are for the young people, gay, lesbian, and heterosexual, who need their support and guidance.

V. FAMILIES OF GAY AND LESBIAN YOUTH

"On reflecting about homosexuality, I've learned that: my religious tradition taught me to believe that my son was a sinner; my medical support system taught me to believe that my son was sick; my educational system taught me that my son was abnormal; my legal system views my son and his partner in an unsanctioned relationship without legal rights and protection that are afforded my married daughter; my family, immediate and extended, provided no acknowledgment or support for having a gay relative in its midst; my major communication sources treated homosexuality as deviant."

—James Genasci, father of a gay son,
testifying at the Public Hearings.

Families, and parents particularly, are profoundly affected when a child or sibling is gay or lesbian. The expected course of family life is changed irrevocably. And the course it takes, the new actions and attitudes it assumes toward the gay/lesbian teen, can mean the difference between life and death.

Gay and lesbian adolescents in the closet

"I still have to come out to my parents, but we have grown distant ... and they hardly know me anymore. I'm afraid of what their reaction might be." —Devin Beringer, 17, testifying at the Public Hearings.

If the teen has not come out to his or her parents, a rift develops in which both family and teen feel separated from each other. The secrets needed to maintain silence pile up like the Berlin Wall, increasing the teen's isolation from his family and his sense of aloneness.

"It cannot get back to my 12-year-old sister that I am anything apart from a carefree, heterosexual high school senior or as my father so eloquently put it, 'The heavens will fall in on your petty life.'" —Zoe Hart, 17, testifying at the Public Hearings.

"Over these past two years, I have seen that she knows what it means not to be able to share this information with parents and friends, and how painful it is." —Happie Byers, grandmother of a lesbian teen, testifying at the Public Hearings.

Out to the family

If the gay/lesbian teen reveals his or her identity, the family unit is often deeply shaken. It must revise its image of the teen, but also of itself as a unit. The family must deal with the many feelings that follow, and the reactions of extended family and community.

Parents testifying at the Governor's Commission on Gay and Lesbian Youth's Public Hearings spoke of being unprepared for the news that their son or daughter was gay or lesbian.

"Society had ill-prepared me to be the father of a gay son. To be brought up in this society is to be brought up homophobic." —James Genasci, testifying at the Public Hearings.

"We began to ask ourselves the guilt-based question 'What did I do wrong?' After all, our Italian-American and Irish-American families were saturated with Roman Catholic doctrine and the cultural imperative of normality. Clearly we had failed and he was somehow defective." —Sandra Bayne, mother of a gay son, testifying at the Public Hearings.

The family in the closet

The family must cope with how the world reacts to them as a family with a gay or lesbian member, as well as to the teen himself/herself. The organization P-FLAG (Parents and Friends of Lesbians and Gays) finds that often families go into the closet when their gay/lesbian child comes out.

"We began, perhaps worst of all, to live the lie. This is the extremely stressful experience of monitoring everything you say lest you reveal what cannot be revealed, and then lying to hide the truth ... Lying breeds self-loathing, so you begin to avoid those to whom you must lie." —Sandra Bayne, testifying at the Public Hearings.

Silence, ignorance, avoidance

Families often have no realistic conception of what it means to be gay or lesbian or to have a loved one who is lesbian or gay. They have been exposed to stereotypes of gays and lesbians and rarely have read accurate books or articles about gay/lesbian people. Three themes which have permeated society's attitudes and treatment of young gays or lesbians are: silence, ignorance, and avoidance. Society usually talks about homosexuality in a pejorative sense and avoids the presence and needs of young gays and lesbians. The result of this atmosphere is a family in denial and in great distress.

Often when families learn that a son or daughter is gay or lesbian, the reaction is shame and guilt. Without support or knowledge, they feel confused and alone.

"In the beginning, I was full of sadness and fear for our son and his partner ... and along with my husband, wondered who would be supportive." —Jean Genasci, mother of a gay son, testifying at the Public Hearings.

Hostility and rejection from family

Some parents turn against their lesbian/gay child in anger and these teens are thrown out of their homes or driven to run away. Sometimes these gay/lesbian adolescents end up on the streets, becoming self-destructive and all too often attempting suicide.

"I got kicked out of my house in July, and at that point there was violence involved. My mother went nuts and came at me with an iron and I ran downstairs and I locked the door and she called the police. The police came and they asked what was going on. And I told them, and my mother started saying that I'm always in Boston with the fags and that I'm doing this and I'm doing that. And he started cracking all kinds of gay jokes and telling me what he would do to his kids if they were gay and he told me that I should leave." —Troix Bettencourt, 18, testifying at the Public Hearings.

Twenty-six percent of young gays and lesbians are forced to leave home because of conflicts over their sexual orientation, according to the U.S. Department of Health and Human Services (Gibson, *Report of the Secretary's Task Force on Youth Suicide*, 1989).

"Then came the moment of truth. My dad wanted an explanation, a reason for my disenrollment from the ROTC, and my very worst fears were realized when I suddenly became persona non grata in my own home." —Chris Collins, University of Massachusetts–Amherst student, testifying at the Public Hearings.

Parallel issues between gay and lesbian adolescents and their families

"We experience the same feelings our children have experienced: the utter confusion over what homosexuality means, the fear of not fitting into a very uniform society, the fear of rejection by our parents and relatives and friends, even the fear of physical harm, and of course AIDS." —Sandra Bayne, testifying at the Public Hearings.

Many of the same issues afflicting young gays and lesbians also afflict their families: isolation, rejection, feelings of failure, disappointment, and rage.

"My family, immediate and extended, provided no acknowledgment or support." —James Genasci.

Suicide and its effect on families

The devastating effect of suicide, or suicide attempts, on the family unit cannot be overestimated. Mary Griffith's son, Bobby, killed himself at age 20 by jumping off an overpass onto a highway. Mary had been a Christian Fundamentalist. When she and her husband found out that Bobby was gay when he was 16, they tried to "cure" him through prayer and a Christian counselor. Since her son's death, Mary has come to regret that her family did not accept Bobby's gay identity.

"We never thought of a gay person as an equal, lovable, and valuable part of God's creation. What a travesty of God's unconditional love ... Had I viewed my son's life with a pure heart, I would have recognized him as a tender spirit in God's eyes." —Mary Griffith, mother of a gay son who committed suicide.

When JoAnne Cardell's sister, Nancy, told her that she was a lesbian, JoAnne responded judgmentally.

"I told Nancy that I thought that gays were disgusting and I couldn't stand the sight of them, and never wanted to be around them again." —JoAnne Cardell, sister, testimony submitted to the Governor's Commission.

When Nancy died from an overdose of drugs in an apparent suicide, JoAnne felt overwhelmed with remorse.

"I now have an unbelievable amount of guilt due to the discriminatory comment I made to her years ago. I can never take back what I said, and this is one of the main reasons I want to do everything I can to help make this world a better place for those who are lesbian, gay, and bisexual ... If families and society could only realize the deep scars they are digging every time there is gay bashing, a life could be saved." —JoAnne Cardell.

Ruth, a mother of a lesbian daughter who killed herself, blames society's ignorance for her daughter's suicide.

"A wonderful child, with an incredible mind, is gone because our society can't accept people who are 'different' from the norm. What an awful waste. I will miss my daughter for the rest of my life. I'll never see her beautiful smile or hear her glorious laugh. I'll never see her play with her sister again. All because of hatred and ignorance. I strongly believe that the seeds of hate are sown early in life. Let's replace them with love, understanding, and compassion. We have no choice: this terrible tragedy will continue to repeat itself and someday it may be your wonderful child who is gone forever." —Ruth, mother of a lesbian daughter who committed suicide; testimony submitted to the Governor's Commission.

Families of gay and lesbian teenagers need help for themselves in dealing both with their feelings and with the prejudice and mythology of the outside world. They need help as well in order to be able to advocate for the physical and emotional safety of their lesbian/gay teen who must navigate through a school and social life made dangerous by those who hate or fear him/her for being different. Parents and families need help in order to alleviate the guilt and shame they feel, and to empower themselves and their son or daughter in this journey.

SUMMARY OF RECOMMENDATIONS FOR SCHOOLS

The Governor's Commission on Gay and Lesbian Youth recommends that school systems create programs and policies to ensure that gay and lesbian students are safe in Massachusetts schools and that they are able to realize fully their potential to learn.

We recommend that Governor Weld, the Department of Education, and the Executive Office of Education support our recommendations for schools and devise a plan for implementing them in secondary schools throughout Massachusetts.

Our five key recommendations for schools are:

1. School policies protecting gay and lesbian students from harassment, violence, and discrimination

School systems should make public commitments to ensure that schools are safe places, free of discrimination, violence, and harassment, for all students, including gay and lesbian youth.

2. Training teachers/counselors/school staff in crisis intervention and violence prevention

Teachers, guidance counselors, and all school staff should be equipped with the training necessary to respond to the needs of gay and lesbian students, including protecting them from harassment and violence, and intervening to prevent suicide and dropping out.

The Higher Education Coordinating Council should facilitate changes in teacher-training standards so that all certified teachers and educators will receive training in issues relevant to the needs and problems faced by gay and lesbian youth. Such training should be a requirement for teacher certification and school accreditation.

3. School-based support groups for gay and straight students

Gay and lesbian students experience intense isolation, putting them at great risk for suicide. Every high school in the Commonwealth should establish a support group where gay and straight students can meet each week and discuss gay and lesbian youth issues. These gay/straight student alliances should have a faculty advisor.

In addition, existing school counselling services should expand their knowledge and resources to meet the needs of gay and lesbian students.

4. Information in school libraries for gay and lesbian adolescents
School libraries are an important resource for students seeking to learn more on any issue. All school libraries should develop a collection of literature, books, films, and pamphlets for students seeking to learn more on gay and lesbian issues. In particular, a collection of gay and lesbian youth resource information should be developed. The school should widely publicize the existence of this literature through displays, posters, etc.

5. Curriculum which includes gay and lesbian issues
Learning about gay and lesbian people, including their experiences and contributions to society, should be integrated into all subject areas. School systems should urge teachers to continue their education in order to integrate gay and lesbian themes and issues into their subject areas.

Each of the above recommendations is explained more fully in the following pages.

RECOMMENDATION ONE:
School policies which protect gay and lesbian students

Written, formal school policies help prevent discrimination, harassment, and verbal abuse of gay and lesbian students and young people perceived to be lesbian or gay. By making schools safe for gay and lesbian youth, we can prevent drop-out that results from students feeling threatened at school. We can also improve the ability of young people to learn.

We recommend that the following policies be formally adopted by schools, and publicized in areas such as student, faculty, and PTA handbooks:

1. Anti-discrimination policies
Schools should include sexual orientation as a protected category in nondiscrimination policies for students and teachers, including teacher contracts.

2. Policies which guarantee equal access to education and school activities

Schools should establish policies which ensure the rights of gay and lesbian students to education and guarantee equal access to all school courses and school activities.

3. Anti-harassment policies and guidelines

1. Schools should adopt and publicize policies which prohibit anti-gay language and harassment on the part of faculty and students.
2. Clear procedures should be established to deal with incidents of anti-gay harassment and violence, including penalties for such behavior.
3. Clear guidelines should be established for dealing with anti-gay epithets and speech.

4. Multicultural and diversity policies

Schools should include gay and lesbian issues within appropriate policies and programs concerning diversity or multiculturalism.

RECOMMENDATION TWO:
Training teachers and counselors in suicide prevention and violence prevention

School professionals must be equipped with the knowledge necessary for meeting the needs of gay and lesbian students in a sensitive and caring manner. Teachers and school counselors must be trained in how to create a safe and inclusive school environment for gay and lesbian students so that suicides, drop-outs, and incidents of harassment and violence can be prevented.

The teacher/counselor training would have a dual focus. The short-term focus would be to provide teachers and counselors with the necessary skills to intervene effectively with gay and lesbian youth who are in crisis. The long-term focus would seek to equip educators with the skills to create a lasting safe and supportive environment in school for gay and lesbian students, so that the need for future crisis intervention would be reduced or eliminated.

We recommend that teachers, counselors, and school staff in Massachusetts public schools be trained in the following:

1. Violence prevention

We recommend that educators be trained in how to intervene when students who are gay or lesbian, or perceived to be gay or lesbian, are harassed or threatened by other students.

2. Crisis intervention

We recommend that educators be trained and learn how to respond to a gay or lesbian student who seeks help because of isolation, or emotional and physical problems.

3. Counselling referrals

We recommend that educators learn how to make appropriate referrals for gay and lesbian students to counselors, including family counselors, and youth-service agencies.

4. Workshops for teachers and school staff

We recommend that all school systems sponsor workshops for teachers and school staff members to learn how to meet the needs of gay and lesbian students. Included in this education process should be a commitment to addressing and eliminating discriminatory attitudes directed against gay and lesbian people in general.

Goals of a workshop for teachers/staff include:
1. Discussing the special needs of gay and lesbian students
2. Learning about health problems of gay and lesbian youth, such as their high risk for suicide
3. Providing participants with resource materials for responding to the needs of gay lesbian students
4. Learning to relate anti-gay discrimination to other forms of prejudice
5. Discussing participants' existing attitudes towards gay and lesbian people
6. Creating a safe environment for gay and lesbian staff members to be open about their sexual orientation.

5. Changes in teacher certification requirements and school accreditation

We recommend that the Higher Education Coordinating Council facilitate and enforce specific changes in teacher-training programs and certification standards. We recommend that to become certified, teachers, counselors, and educators be required to receive training in issues relevant to the needs of gay and lesbian students. Similarly, schools should be required to schedule in-service diversity trainings in order to receive accreditation from the appropriate professional associations.

RECOMMENDATION THREE:
School-based support groups
for gay and straight students

Students are best supported by other students. Isolation and loneliness on the part of gay and lesbian students can lead to suicide attempts, run-away, drop-out, and a host of emotional and physical problems. Weekly support groups for gay and lesbian students, and any other students who want to talk about gay and lesbian issues, help to counter isolation and to give an ongoing voice to young people who need to be able to talk about their feelings, and about their identity.

Gay/straight alliances, and groups such as PROJECT 10, are effective in-school support groups. We recommend that these kinds of groups be established and supported by the administration in every high school in the Commonwealth.

We also recommend the following:

1. Groups open to all students

Support groups should be open to all students, including self-identified gay and lesbian youth, heterosexual students supportive of their gay and lesbian peers, and any student wishing to discuss lesbian/gay issues in a safe and confidential environment.

2. Faculty advisor

A faculty advisor should be appointed to attend each meeting, listen to students, and communicate their needs to the administration. School personnel with personal experience, such as self-identified gay and lesbian teachers, heterosexual teachers with gay/lesbian friends or family, or the like, should be sought out for this role.

The faculty advisor should undergo extensive, in-depth professional training on the needs of gay and lesbian youth. Appropriate compensation should be offered for this role.

3. Wide publicity of group's existence

The existence of a gay/straight alliance in a school should be widely publicized within the school so that all students know of the group's existence and purpose. Publicity should take the form of pamphlets, information in student and faculty handbooks, posters and flyers, announcements by teachers, etc.

4. Student support through school counselors

In addition to student support and discussion groups, we recommend that school counselors be trained to provide support and information for gay and lesbian youth in the school setting.

We have three specific recommendations for school counselors:

1. All school counselors, nurses, and social workers should receive training concerning gay and lesbian youth issues from professionals in their field.
2. The availability of counselling services for gay and lesbian students should be made known through publicity in the school such as posters, student handbooks, and announcements, so that a welcoming environment is created in the counselling setting.
3. Appropriate and timely referrals should be made for young people whose needs cannot be met within the school's counselling resources.

RECOMMENDATION FOUR:
Information in school libraries
for gay and lesbian adolescents

Young people need to have access to resources and information about gay and lesbian youth issues in school libraries. Information should include books, videos, pamphlets, and other materials for use by students, parents, and teachers. Information should be available which provides for referrals to appropriate counselling and youth-service agencies which are trained in dealing with the needs of gay and lesbian adolescents.

We recommend the following:

1. School libraries should have a special, easily recognizable section of books and materials related to gay and lesbian issues.
2. Confidential sign-out procedures should be implemented so that students may use these resources without feeling a need to make a public statement.
3. School libraries should purchase films concerning gay and lesbian people in general, and gay and lesbian youth in particu-

lar, which are appropriate for viewing by the entire student body and by faculty.

4. School libraries should periodically display books and materials about gay and lesbian issues in a highly visible way.
5. School librarians should develop a reading list of books in the library on gay and lesbian issues which they can provide to teachers for inclusion in class reading lists.
6. Libraries should display a well-researched guide to resources for gay and lesbian youth, including community-based lesbian and gay youth groups such as BAGLY (the Boston Alliance of Gay and Lesbian Youth) and P-FLAG (Parents and Friends of Lesbians and Gays).

RECOMMENDATION FIVE:
Curriculum which includes gay and lesbian issues

The classroom is the heart of the school experience. Discussion of gay and lesbian issues, and recognition of the contribution of gay people to history and to modern society, should be integrated into all subject areas and departments in an age-appropriate fashion.

We recommend the following:

1. Inclusive human development education, which addresses issues of sexual orientation, should be available to all students.
2. Students should be introduced to lesbian and gay culture in a variety of contexts, such as literature, history, the arts, and family life.
3. Biases in existing curriculum, such as the exclusive use of opposite-sex couples in math or foreign language exercises, should be redressed.
4. Diversity programs, which address a variety of prejudices such as those against gay and lesbian people, women, and people of color, should be instituted and available to all students.
5. Academic departments should research ways to include the experiences and contributions of gay and lesbian people as they pertain to their discipline. Each department should set goals and timetables by which to achieve these curriculum changes, with regular assessment of departmental progress by relevant administrators.

6. School systems should encourage and support teachers attending conferences and furthering their education about gay and lesbian issues relevant to their subject area.

SUMMARY OF RECOMMENDATIONS
FOR FAMILIES OF GAY AND LESBIAN YOUTH

We recommend that Governor Weld, the Department of Education, and the Executive Office of Education support our recommendations for families of gay and lesbian youth and work in concert with the Commission to provide the appropriate services and resources.

Our recommendations for helping families of gay and lesbian youth are:

1. Peer-counselling groups in the P-FLAG (Parents and Friends of Lesbians and Gays) model and, in times of crisis, family counselling in school

We recommend that the Department of Education support both long-term and short-term family and peer-group counselling for family members of young gays and lesbians. Such counselling should be supported in the school and within the community.

2. Education of families through information in public libraries

We recommend that all public libraries develop and display collections of up-to-date books as well as information on issues relating to gay and lesbian youth and their families. We also recommend that the Department of Education develop a resource guide for families of gay and lesbian youth.

3. Parent speakers bureaus to advocate for gay and lesbian youth in schools

Families can play an active role in working to make schools safe for gay and lesbian youth and to prevent suicide attempts and dropout. We recommend that Governor Weld designate a parent in each school district who will advocate for gay and lesbian youth in schools, and with other parents and educators, make panel presentations in the community.

Each of the above recommendations is explained more fully in the following pages.

RECOMMENDATION ONE:
Peer counselling in the P-FLAG model
and family counselling in school

We recommend that the Department of Education support and develop organizations throughout Massachusetts which offer peer-group counselling for families of gay and lesbian youth. These should be ongoing, long-term support and discussion groups for families of gays and lesbians.

The organization P-FLAG (Parents and Friends of Lesbians and Gays) offers a model for this kind of counselling where families of gays and lesbians provide help and understanding for other families. Information on the availability of groups such as these should be disseminated through PTAs and pupil service coordinators at schools.

The Department of Education should also support short-term family counselling as requested by families of gay and lesbian youth or by the youth themselves within the school setting. These meetings would seek to open up communication among family members in order to diminish family strains and prevent isolation of the gay or lesbian youth.

RECOMMENDATION TWO:
Education of families through information in public libraries

We recommend that public libraries develop and maintain an up-to-date collection of books and information on issues relating to gay and lesbian youth and families of gays or lesbians, as well as books on gay and lesbian issues in general. Parents and families of gays and lesbians would play a role in the selection process. In addition, we recommend that public libraries include movies on gay and lesbian themes in their regular screening schedules and advertise them widely in the local community.

We also recommend that the Department of Education develop a resource guide for families of gay and lesbian youth to be distributed to every school principal and superintendent, to School Committees and PTA members, and to all school and public libraries. The resource guide should also be distributed to public clinics, hospitals, and a variety of human service agencies.

RECOMMENDATION THREE:
Parent speakers bureaus to advocate for gay and lesbian youth in schools

We recommend that Governor Weld designate a parent liaison in every school district to work with the Commission and to advocate for services for gay and lesbian youth in schools. The parent would work to ensure a safe and supportive environment for young gays and lesbians within our public school system.

The Department of Education, in concert with the parent liaison, should create and support parent speakers bureaus throughout the state. These parent speakers bureaus would perform two functions: outreach and advocacy in the larger community, and education of groups within the school community. The bureaus would also communicate regularly with local School Committees and PTAs.

RECOMMENDATIONS TO STATE AGENCIES AND TO THE MASSACHUSETTS LEGISLATURE

The Governor's Commission on Gay and Lesbian Youth is making recommendations to three state agencies and to the Massachusetts Legislature so that our recommendations for schools and families can be effectively implemented. The Department of Education, the Executive Office of Education, and the Massachusetts Commission Against Discrimination (MCAD) together can play a powerful role as a catalyst in guiding school systems to learn about the problems of gay and lesbian students and in working to create a safe learning environment for them. The Massachusetts Legislature can guarantee the rights of gay and lesbian youth to public education.

State government can have an impact on local schools by:
• serving as a voice of influence
• compiling and disseminating policies and guidelines
• compiling and disseminating information and resources
• conducting outreach programs to inform and foster action

The Commission is making a total of ten recommendations to state agencies and the legislature. Our recommendations are explained on the following pages.

Recommendations to the
Massachusetts Department of Education

1. Sponsor training for teachers, families, and students to learn about the problems of gay and lesbian youth

We recommend that the Department of Education co-sponsor conferences and workshops with the Commission to educate teachers and families about how to meet the needs of gay and lesbian students. The training should focus on suicide intervention, drop-out prevention, substance abuse prevention, violence prevention, and on making schools safe for all students, gay, lesbian, or heterosexual.

2. Make presentations to School Committee Associations concerning the problems faced by gay and lesbian youth

We recommend that the Department of Education conduct presentations and workshops at meetings or conferences of School Committee Associations about the problems and needs of gay and lesbian students. The Commission's recommendations should also be presented at these meetings. There should be at least one parent and one teenager in each group which presents to the School Committee members.

3. Develop and disseminate a yellow pages resource book about gay and lesbian youth

We recommend that the Department of Education develop three separate versions of a resource book about services and support for gay and lesbian youth. Versions should be developed for students, for teachers, and for families.

These resource guides should be sent to school libraries, public libraries, PTA members, school committee members, school principals, and guidance counselors, as well as to teachers.

Recommendations to the Executive Office of Education

1. Develop and promote anti-harassment policies and guidelines for protecting gay and lesbian students

We recommend that the Executive Office of Education conduct a statewide campaign, in cooperation with the Department of Education, to promote adoption of anti-harassment policies and guidelines which will protect all students, gay, lesbian, and heterosexual, in the

Commonwealth. Guidelines should include suggestions for disciplinary action as well as procedures for handling incidents of anti-gay violence.

2. Develop and promote school policies that will guarantee gay and lesbian students equal rights to an education

We recommend that the Executive Office of Education conduct a statewide campaign, in cooperation with the Department of Education, to urge school systems to adopt and publicize policies which guarantee the rights of gay and lesbian students to an education. These policies should include protecting the rights of gay and lesbian students to participate in all courses of study as well as in school activities.

3. Research the problems of gay and lesbian students and the needs of teachers and families

We recommend that statewide research focusing on the problems faced in school by gay and lesbian students be conducted by the Executive Office of Education and that the results be widely publicized. The attitudes and needs of teachers, as well as those of family members of lesbian and gay adolescents, should be researched.

Recommendations to the Massachusetts Commission Against Discrimination (MCAD)

1. Conduct outreach to teachers and school personnel to inform them of their rights under the gay civil rights law

Many teachers and school professionals live in fear of losing their livelihood because they are unaware of their legal rights, or because their school administration has not explicitly made a commitment to protecting the civil rights of gay and lesbian educators. We recommend that the MCAD conduct a statewide outreach program to inform teachers, principals, and school personnel about the provisions of the state's Gay and Lesbian Civil Rights Law, which was enacted in 1989. This outreach campaign should include informing educators about the legal remedies available to them.

2. Sponsor anti-discrimination awareness programs in schools for all students to learn about the gay civil rights law

We recommend that the MCAD make presentations in schools across the state to teach students about the state's Gay and Lesbian

Civil Rights Law, including the history of the law's passage, its impact on Massachusetts, and the provisions of the law.

3. Sponsor legislation to extend MCAD's jurisdiction to include complaints of education discrimination

We recommend that the MCAD sponsor legislation to amend the Massachusetts General Laws to increase the scope of its jurisdiction to include investigation and prosecution of complaints of education discrimination, including but not limited to sexual orientation discrimination.

Recommendation to the Massachusetts Legislature

1. Pass the bill entitled "An Act to Prohibit Discrimination Against Students in Public Schools on the Basis of Sexual Orientation"

We recommend that the Massachusetts Legislature enact and Governor Weld sign into law an amendment to section 5 of chapter 76 of the General Laws. The phrase "sexual orientation" shall be added to the existing law. The law would then read as follows:

"No person shall be excluded from or discriminated against in admission to a public school of any town, or in obtaining the advantages, privileges, and courses of study of such public school on account of race, color, sex, religion, national origin, or sexual orientation."

APPENDIX A: SURVEY OF HIGH SCHOOL STUDENTS

In February 1993, the Governor's Commission on Gay and Lesbian Youth surveyed students at Lincoln-Sudbury Regional High School about their attitudes towards gay, lesbian, and bisexual issues. Approximately 400 students completed the surveys, which asked students to identify themselves by gender, grade level, and age. Respondents were also asked to answer twelve multiple-choice questions, and were given an opportunity to add any additional comments related to the issues on the survey. We present here the results of five of the questions on the survey, along with the comments of some of the students. The verbatim questions and multiple-choice answers are shown for each question. Full survey results are available from the Governor's Commission.

Student comments

"By having a club those who were gay would be revealed and then ridiculed by other students ... Prejudices are things that we may try to ignore, and to deny. We may say we are not prejudiced, and make ourselves believe that. But as people we are constantly making assumptions and forming ideas of others. It is a sad truth."

—Male, 17 years old

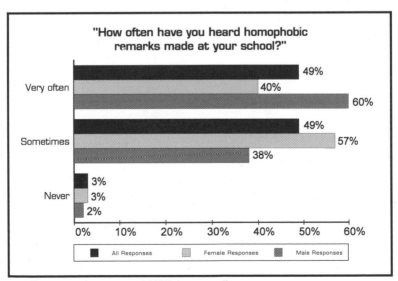

NOTE: Category total may not equal 100% due to rounding.
SOURCE: Survey of students at Lincoln-Sudbury Regional High School, February 1993, N=402

"...just keep them out of my sight and away from me."
                                        —Male, 16 years old

"I hate them."   —Male, 16 years old

"I believe that homosexuals and bisexuals are living in sin. The person should not be discriminated against, but helped with the forgiveness of their sin by God."   —Female, 17 years old

"I think that it is right to have support groups if the people were teased or need to get it in the open. But I think it should be treated like any club; if they get rowdy they should discontinue the club. No special treatment because that makes people think they are different."
                                        —Female, 14 years old

"Discrimination is wrong in any form."   —Male, 14 years old

"Many people I know are homosexual. It is accepted even though it provides for some interesting conversation."
                                        —Female, 17 years old

"I am not gay but I have a friend who is & I think it is really mean when people make fun of him."   —Female, 14 years old

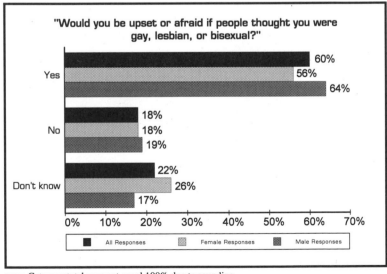

"Would you be upset or afraid if people thought you were gay, lesbian, or bisexual?"

NOTE: Category total may not equal 100% due to rounding.
SOURCE: Survey of students at Lincoln-Sudbury Regional High School, February 1993, N=402

"Learning about the gay and lesbian community should start at a young age. Some people I know are already prejudiced against homosexuals because they were never exposed to any information about them when they were younger."   —Female, 16 years old

"I believe that this topic should be openly and more frequently discussed in schools. I believe that discrimination, of any kind is wrong. Educating people may help solve this problem."
—Female, 18 years old

"I think it is important that in high schools students & teachers have open discussions on this topic."   —Female, 18 years old

"People should be taught more in school about the subject."
—Female, 14 years old

"I myself am going into the military next year and in response to the recent controversy surrounding gays/lesbians in the military — I think it is great if anybody wants to go into the military. They are certainly entitled to the same rights as I am."
—Female, 18 years old

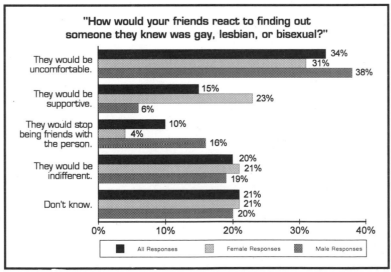

NOTE: Category total may not equal 100% due to rounding.
SOURCE: Survey of students at Lincoln-Sudbury Regional High School, February 1993, N=402

"I think that gays and lesbians shouldn't be allowed in the Army. I don't think that they should be allowed to teach, and the students if gay or a lesbian should keep it to themselves, and let it be known to only them, and not the rest of society."   —Female, 15 years old

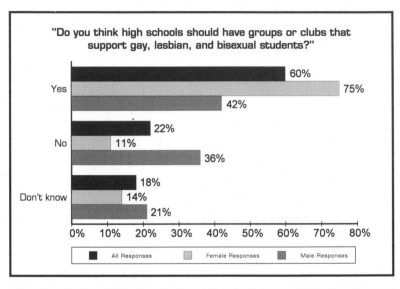

"Do you think high schools should have groups or clubs that support gay, lesbian, and bisexual students?"

Yes
- 60%
- 75%
- 42%

No
- 22%
- 11%
- 36%

Don't know
- 18%
- 14%
- 21%

■ All Responses   ▨ Female Responses   ▩ Male Responses

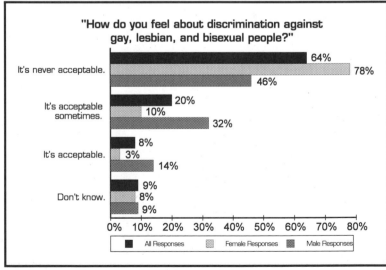

"How do you feel about discrimination against gay, lesbian, and bisexual people?"

It's never acceptable.
- 64%
- 78%
- 46%

It's acceptable sometimes.
- 20%
- 10%
- 32%

It's acceptable.
- 8%
- 3%
- 14%

Don't know.
- 9%
- 8%
- 9%

■ All Responses   ▨ Female Responses   ▩ Male Responses

NOTE: Category total may not equal 100% due to rounding.
SOURCE: Survey of students at Lincoln-Sudbury Regional High School, February 1993, N=402

APPENDIX B: SURVEY OF COMMUNITY GROUPS AND SCHOOL GAY/STRAIGHT ALLIANCES

This survey was developed and conducted by the Boston Alliance of Gay and Lesbian Youth (BAGLY) in cooperation with the Governor's Commission on Gay and Lesbian Youth. The survey was developed to gauge what high school life is like for students who are lesbian, gay, or bisexual. This survey was distributed at seven community-based lesbian and gay youth groups and eight school-based

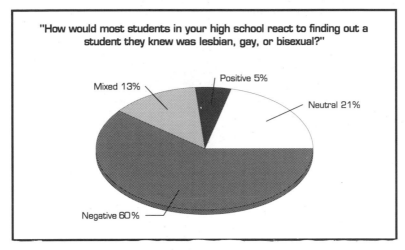

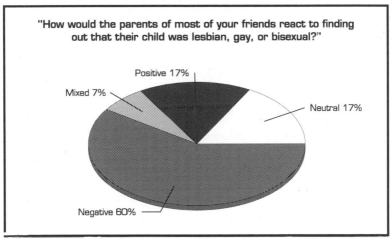

NOTE: Category total may not equal 100% due to rounding.
SOURCE: Survey of youth from community groups and school-based gay/straight alliances, N=218

gay/straight alliances across Massachusetts. It contained 33 questions; results of 4 of them are presented here. The 218 youth responding to the survey ranged in age from 13 to 23.

Community groups surveyed included BAGLY, the Brockton Regional Alliance of Gay and Lesbian Youth (BRAGLY), the Framingham Alliance of Gay and Lesbian Youth (FRAGLY), the North Shore Alliance of Gay and Lesbian Youth (NAGLY), Pioneer Valley Youth Group, the Supporters of Worcester Area Gay and Lesbian Youth

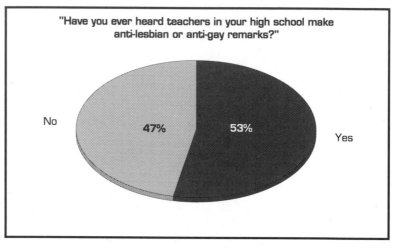

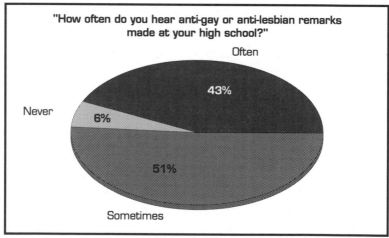

NOTE: Category total may not equal 100% due to rounding.
SOURCE: Survey of youth from community groups and school-based gay/straight alliances, N=218

(SWAGLY), and the Lowell Gay Youth Group. School-based groups were from Brookline High School, Cambridge Rindge & Latin High School, Lincoln-Sudbury Regional High School, Newton South High School, Buckingham Browne & Nichols School, Concord Academy, Milton Academy, and Noble & Greenough School.

APPENDIX C: EXECUTIVE ORDER NO. 325

WHEREAS, this Administration is committed to protecting the physical, emotional, and psychological health and well-being of all young people in the Commonwealth; and

WHEREAS, the U.S. Department of Health and Human Services, in its 1989 *Report of the Secretary's Task Force on Youth Suicide,* estimates that 30% of completed youth suicides annually are by gay and lesbian youth; and

WHEREAS, the same report states that suicide is the leading cause of death for gay and lesbian youth; and

WHEREAS, the 1989 Report estimates that 26% of young gays and lesbians are forced to leave home because of conflicts over their sexual identity and that gay and lesbian youth form a large component of the homeless youth population; and

WHEREAS, this Administration is committed to abolishing harassment, violence, and discrimination against young people because of their real or perceived sexual orientation; and

WHEREAS, Massachusetts has been and continues to be in the forefront of the national movement to end discrimination and prejudice directed at gays and lesbians; and

WHEREAS, many of the problems facing gay and lesbian youth are within the purview of state government and can be corrected by promulgation of information, training, and the implementation and diffusion of formal guidelines and state policy; and

WHEREAS, the health of the Commonwealth is served by strengthening the physical and emotional health of both individuals and their families;

NOW, THEREFORE, I, William F. Weld, Governor of the Commonwealth of Massachusetts, by virtue of the authority vested in me as Supreme Executive Magistrate, do hereby create the Governor's Commission on Gay and Lesbian Youth and order as follows:

1. The Commission shall consist of at least sixteen (16) members who shall serve without compensation. The Governor shall designate the chair of the Commission. The membership of the Commission shall include at least one parent of a gay or lesbian person; one high school student; one college student; one representative from an educational institution; and one representative of the mental health profession.

2. The Commission shall meet on a quarterly basis with the Secretary of Education, Secretary of Health and Human Services, Public Health Commissioner, and the Secretary of Communities and Development or their designees and shall advise the Executive Office of Health and Human Services on an ongoing basis.

3. The Commission shall investigate the utilization of resources from both the public and private sectors to enhance and improve the ability of state agencies to provide services to gay and lesbian youth.

4. The Commission shall report to the Governor and make recommendations to the Governor relating to the concerns of gay and lesbian youth. The report shall be filed with the Governor on or before September 30, 1992.

Given at the Executive Chamber in Boston this 10th day of February in the year of our Lord one thousand nine hundred and ninety-two.

William F. Weld, Governor
Commonwealth of Massachusetts
Michael Joseph Connolly
Secretary of the Commonwealth

MEMBERS OF THE GOVERNOR'S COMMISSION ON GAY AND LESBIAN YOUTH

David LaFontaine, Canton: Chair
Alice Foley, Provincetown: Vice-Chair
Jessica Byers, Cambridge: Education Committee Co-Chair
Al Ferreira, Leominster: Education Committee Co-Chair
Doris Held, Cambridge: Education Committee Co-Chair

Kevin Jennings, Cambridge: Education Committee Co-Chair
Jerry Cheney, Worcester: Human Services Committee Co-Chair
Sterling Stowell, Cambridge: Human Services Committee Co-Chair

The Reverend Stewart Barns, Cambridge
Sharon Bergman, Amherst
Dean Bruno, Stoneham
Luann Conaty, Northborough
Bill Conley, Wilbraham
Harold Dufour-Anderson, Cambridge
Marshall Forstein, Jamaica Plain
Alexander Gray, Boston
Holly Gunner, Newton
Steve Johnson, Boston
Cynthia Lanane, Allston
Abner Mason, Boston
Enrique Maysonet, Worcester
Vincent McCarthy, Boston
Margaret O'Neill, Quincy
Dale Orlando, Lynn
Stephen Perreault, Cambridge
Michael Savage, Boston

BIBLIOGRAPHY

Bell, A., and Weinberg, M. (1978). *Homosexualities: A study of diversity among men and women.* New York: Simon & Schuster.

Centers for Disease Control (1991, September 20). Attempted suicide among high-school students — United States, 1990. In U.S. Department of Health and Human Services, *Health Objectives for the Nation,* Vol. 40, No. 37, pp. 433–435.

Fifield, L. (1975). *On my way to nowhere: Alienated, isolated, drunk.* Los Angeles: Gay Community Services Center.

Finn, P., and McNeil, T. (1987). *The response of the criminal justice system to bias crime: An exploratory view.* Washington, DC: U.S. Department of Justice.

Fisher, P., and Shaffer, D. (1990). Facts about suicide: A review of national mortality statistics and records. In M.J. Rotheram-Borus, J. Bradley, and N. Obolensky (Eds.), *Planning to live: Evaluating and treating suicidal teens in community settings.* Tulsa: University of Oklahoma Press.

Gibson, Paul (1989). Gay male and lesbian youth suicide. In *Report of the Secretary's Task Force on Youth Suicide: Vol. 3. Prevention and interventions in youth suicide* (pp. 100–142). Washington, DC: U.S. Department of Health and Human Services.

Goff, J.L (1990, Fall). Sexual confusion among certain college males. *Adolescence, 25*(99).

Harbeck, Karen (1992). *Coming out of the classroom closet: Gay and lesbian students, teachers, and curricula.* Binghamton, NY: Harrington Park Press.

Hendin, H. (1982). Suicide and homosexuality. Chapter 5 of *Suicide in America.* New York: W.W. Norton.

Herek, Gregory (1984). Beyond "homophobia": A social psychological perspective on attitudes toward lesbians and gay men." *Journal of Homosexuality.*

Hetrick, E.S., and Martin, A.D. (1988). *Hetrick-Martin Institute violence report.* New York: The Institute for the Protection of Lesbian and Gay Youth.

Hunter, Joyce, and Schaecher, Robert (1987, Spring). Stresses on lesbian and gay adolescents in schools. *Social Work in Education.*

Hunter, Joyce (1990). Violence against lesbian and gay male youths. *Journal of Interpersonal Violence.*

Jacobs, J. (1971). *Adolescent suicide.* New York: Wiley.

Jay, K., and Young, A. (1977). *The gay report: Lesbian and gay men speak out about their sexual experiences and lifestyles.* New York: Summit.

Kourany, R.F.C. (1987, Summer). Suicide among homosexual adolescents. *Journal of Homosexuality, 13*(4).

Kruds, G. (1991). Gay and lesbian homeless/street youth: Special issues and concerns. *Journal of Adolescent Health.*

Maltsberger, John T. (1986). *Suicide risk: The formulation of clinical judgment.* New York: New York University Press.

Martin, A.D. (1982). Learning to hide: The socialization of the gay adolescent. *Adolescent Psychiatry, 10.*

McManus, Marilyn C. (1991, Spring/Summer). Serving gay and lesbian youth. *Focal Point.*

National Gay and Lesbian Task Force (1984). *National anti-gay/lesbian victimization report.* New York: Author.

Remafedi, Gary (1985). *Male homosexuality: The adolescent's perspective.* Minneapolis: Adolescent Health Program, University of Minnesota.

Remafedi, G., Farrow, J.A., and Deisher, R.W. (1991). Risk factors for attempted suicide in gay and bisexual youth. *Pediatrics, 87.*

Rich, C.L., Fowler, F.C., Young, D., and Blenkush, M. (1986). San Diego suicide study: Comparison of gay to straight males. *Suicide and Life-Threatening Behavior, 16*(4).

Schneider, S., Farberow, N., and Kruks, G. (1989). Suicidal behavior in adolescent and young adult gay men. *Suicide and Life-Threatening Behavior, 19*(4).

Sears, James (1988). *Attitudes, experiences, and feelings of guidance counselors about working with homosexual students* (Document #296210). New Orleans: American Educational Research Association.

Sears, James (1989). *Personal feelings and professional attitudes of prospective teachers toward homosexuality and homosexual students: Research findings and curriculum recommendations* (Document #312222). San Francisco: American Educational Research Association.

Sears, James (1991). *Growing up gay in the South: Race, gender and journeys of the spirit.* New York: Haworth Press.

Sears, James (1991, September). Helping students understand and accept sexual diversity. *Educational Leadership.*

Shaffer, D., Garland, A., Gould, M., Fisher, P., and Trautman, P. (1988). Preventing teenage suicide: A critical review. *Journal of the American Academy of Child Psychiatry, 27*(6).

Yates, G.L., MacKenzie, R., and Pennbridge, J. (1988). A risk profile comparison of runaway and non-runaway youth. *American Journal of Public Health.*

Other books of interest from
ALYSON
PUBLICATIONS

TWO TEENAGERS IN TWENTY, edited by Ann Heron, cloth, $18.00. Twelve years after compiling *One Teenager in Ten,* the first book ever to allow dozens of teenagers to describe what it's like to be gay or lesbian, Ann Heron asked for stories from a new generation. She found that their sense of isolation and despair runs every bit as deep as a decade ago. *Two Teenagers in Twenty* combines these new voices with many essays from her first book. It will greatly ease the way for teenagers just now coming out, and the adults who seek to support them.

BECOMING VISIBLE, edited by Kevin Jennings, $10.00. Drawing from both primary and secondary sources, this reader covers more than 2000 years of history and a diverse range of cultures. Designed for classroom use with students from ninth grade through college, *Becoming Visible* contains classroom activities and curriculum suggestions to help teachers incorporate this material into existing classes. General readers seeking insight into gay and lesbian history will also welcome this book.

TRYING HARD TO HEAR YOU, by Sandra Scoppettone, $8.00. Sixteen-year-old Camilla Crawford tells about a crucial summer in which her close-knit summer theater group discovers that two of its members are gay. By the end of summer, she writes, "two of us were going to suffer like we never had before, and none of us would ever be the same again."

THE ALYSON ALMANAC, by Alyson Publications, $10.00. *The Alyson Almanac* is the most complete reference book available about the lesbian and gay community — and also the most entertaining. Here are brief biographies of some 300 individuals from throughout history; a report card for every member of Congress; significant dates from our history; addresses and phone numbers for major organizations, periodicals, and hotlines; and much more.

ALL-AMERICAN BOYS, by Frank Mosca, $6.00. "I've known I was gay since I was thirteen. Does that surprise you? It didn't me. Actually, it was the most natural thing in the world. I thought everyone was. At least until I hit high school. That's when I finally realized all those faggot and dyke stories referred to people like me..." So begins this story of a teenage love affair that should have been simple — but wasn't.

SOCIETY AND THE HEALTHY HOMOSEXUAL, by George Weinberg, $8.00. Rarely has anyone communicated so much in a single word, as Dr. George Weinberg did when he introduced the term *homophobia* to a wide audience. With a single stroke of the pen, he turned the tables on centuries of prejudice. Homosexuality is healthy, said Weinberg: homophobia is a sickness. Weinberg examines the causes of homophobia and shows how gay people can overcome its pervasive influence.

REVELATIONS, edited by Adrien Saks and Wayne Curtis, $8.00. For most gay men, one critical moment stands out as a special time in the coming-out process. It may be a special friendship, or a sexual episode, or a book or movie that communicates the right message at the right time. In *Revelations,* twenty-two men of varying ages and backgrounds describe this moment of truth.

TESTIMONIES, edited by Karen Barber and Sarah Holmes, $8.00. More than twenty women of widely varying backgrounds and ages recount their journeys toward self-discovery. The stories portray the women's efforts to develop a lesbian identity, explore their sexuality, and build a community with other lesbians.

YOUNG, GAY AND PROUD!, edited by Sasha Alyson, $4.00. One high school student in ten is gay. Here is the first book to ever address the needs of that often-invisible minority. It helps young people deal with questions like: Am I really gay? What would my friends think if I told them? Should I tell my parents? Does anybody else feel the way I do? Other sections discuss health concerns and sexuality, and offer suggestions for further reading.

IN THE LIFE, edited by Joseph Beam, $9.00. When writer and activist Joseph Beam became frustrated that so little gay literature spoke to him as a black gay man, he did something about it: the result was *In the Life,* an anthology which takes its name from a black slang expression for "gay." Here, thirty-three writers and artists explore in stories, essays, poetry, and artwork what it means to be doubly different — black and gay — in modern America.

COMING OUT RIGHT, by Wes Muchmore and William Hanson, $8.00. Every gay man can recall the first time he stepped into a gay bar. That difficult step often represents the transition from a life of secrecy and isolation into a world of unknowns. The transition will be easier for men who have this recently updated book. Here, many facets of gay life are spelled out for the newcomer, including: coming out at work; gay health and the AIDS crisis; and the unique problems faced by men who are coming out when they're under eighteen or over thirty.